The
Collapse
of
Communism

The
Collapse
of
Communism

Edited by

Lee Edwards

HOOVER INSTITUTION PRESS
Stanford University   Stanford, California

www-hoover.stanford.edu

Hoover Institution Press Publication No. 473

Copyright © 2000 by the Board of Trustees of the
Leland Stanford Junior University

First printing, 1999
06 05 04 03 02 01 00   9 8 7 6 5 4 3 2 1

Manufactured in the United States of America

The paper used in this publication meets the minimum requirements
of American National Standard for Information Sciences—Permanence
of Paper for Printed Library Materials, ANSI Z39.48–1984. ⊗

Library of Congress Cataloging-in-Publication Data
The collapse of communism / edited by Lee Edwards.
        p.   cm.
Includes bibliographical references and index.
ISBN 0-8179-9812-8
    1. Communism—History—20th century.   I. Edwards, Lee.
HX40.C663   1999
335.43—dc21   99-048364
                                                        CIP

CONTENTS

FOREWORD

THE COLLAPSE OF COMMUNISM, epitomized by the fall of the
Berlin Wall, is one of the defining features of the second half
of the twentieth century. In the 1980s, Eastern Europe was
under the control of communism. The dissolution of the Soviet Union changed everything. In the wake of the euphoria
surrounding the fall of this totalitarian political and economic
system, one is concerned that socialism will creep back into
parts of Europe. It is our view that we should remind ourselves
of the vagaries of communism in the hope that individual,
political, and economic freedom will become entrenched in
the former Soviet bloc.

The Hoover Institution has a long record of studying communism and collecting materials from East and Central Europe. The many archival treasures and research materials we
possess in the Hoover Institution Archives include recent ac-
quisitions of the entire broadcast archives of Radio Fee Eu-
rope/Radio Liberty and microfilm of more than twelve million
pages of documentation from the Soviet Communist Party Archives.

In the *Collapse of Communism*, nine authors, immensely respected in the field, analyze communism in the twentieth century. The volume was conceived by Lee Edwards, who assembled this outstanding group of scholars to dissect why the system failed. They examine facts, myths, and theories, as well as politics and economics. This volume is comprehensive and, in our view, an indispensable guide and handbook for those interested in learning more about what led to the demise of communism in Europe. Not forgetting that experience is important for the future of freedom.

We want to thank Lee Edwards profusely for his enthusiasm and perseverance in assembling this volume in record time so it would be available by the tenth anniversary of the fall of the wall. It is a terrific collection.

We would like to thank Joan and David Traitel for their significant ongoing support of the Hoover Institution. David is a beacon not only in articulating the importance of history but in pushing the Institution to disseminate its scholarship, accurately portraying truth, not revisionism. David perpetually reminds us that we cannot forget what happened during the era of communism, lest we risk its return.

We call to your attention two other Hoover volumes. *CNN's Cold War: Issues and Controversy* (Hoover Press, 1999), edited by Arnold Beichman, assesses CNN's cold war documentary television program and related book, which generated significant controversy among some historians of the cold war period. In addition, Peter Schweizer edited *The Fall of the Berlin Wall* (Hoover Press, 1999). This volume focuses on the causes and consequences of the end of the cold war and complements the *Collapse of Communism*.

John Raisian
Director
Hoover Institution
Stanford University

ACKNOWLEDGMENTS

THIS BOOK would not have been possible without the generous support and professional assistance of the Hoover Institution, led by its inestimable director, John Raisian. I am deeply indebted to Patricia Baker, executive director of the Hoover Press, and her dedicated colleagues for accomplishing a not so minor miracle—publishing *The Collapse of Communism* in just two months. I also wish to thank Edwin J. Feulner, president of the Heritage Foundation, for his continuing support and Teri Ruddy for her editorial assistance. As always, I wish to acknowledge the contributions of Lev E. Dobriansky, Zbigniew Brzezinski, Robert Conquest, Richard Pipes, and the other founders who have helped to make the Victims of Communism Memorial Foundation a reality.

CONTRIBUTORS

ANDRZEJ BRZESKI is a professor of economics emeritus at the University of California, Davis. A former prisoner in the Soviet Gulag, his latest publication (with Enrico Colombatto) is "Can Eastern Europe Catch Up?" (*Post-Communist Economies*)

ZBIGNIEW BRZEZINSKI, formerly national security adviser to President Carter, is a counselor at the Center for Strategic and International Studies and a professor of American foreign policy at the School of Advanced International Studies, the Johns Hopkins University.

ROBERT CONQUEST is a senior research fellow and scholar-curator of the Russian and CIS Collection at the Hoover Institution. His latest book is *Reflections on a Ravaged Century* (W. W. Norton).

BRIAN CROZIER is a distinguished visiting fellow at the Hoover Institution. He has been a writer and analyst of international affairs for more than fifty years. His latest book is *The Rise and Fall of the Soviet Empire* (Prima).

LEE EDWARDS is the president of the Victims of Communism Memorial Foundation. He teaches politics at the Catholic University of America and is a senior fellow at the Heritage Foundation.

PAUL HOLLANDER is a professor of sociology at the University of Massachusetts (Amherst) and a fellow at the Davis Center for Russian Studies at Harvard University. His latest book is *Political Will and Personal Belief: The Decline and Fall of Soviet Communism* (Yale University Press).

MARTIN MALIA is a professor of history emeritus at the University of California, Berkeley. His latest book is *Russia under Western Eyes: From the Bronze Horseman to the Lenin Mausoleum* (Harvard University Press).

MICHAEL NOVAK is the George Frederick Jewett Scholar in Religion, Philosophy, and Public Policy and director of Social and Political Studies at the American Enterprise Institute. His latest book is *On Cultivating Liberty: Reflections on Moral Ecology* (Roman & Littlefield).

RICHARD PIPES, director of East European and Soviet Affairs on the National Security Council under President Reagan, is Research Professor of History at Harvard University. His latest book is *Property and Freedom* (Alfred A. Knopf).

INTRODUCTION

Lee Edwards

COMMUNISM, the dark tyranny that controlled more than forty nations and was responsible for the deaths of an estimated 100 million victims during the twentieth century, suddenly collapsed a decade ago without a shot being fired. In just two years—from 1989 to 1991—the Berlin Wall fell, the Soviet Union disintegrated, and Marxism-Leninism was dumped unceremoniously on the ash heap of history. There was dancing in the street and champagne toasts on top of the Brandenberg Gate, and then most of the world—including many in the academy—got on with living without bothering to ask relevant questions such as, Why did communism collapse? Why did a totalitarian system that appeared to be so militarily and economically strong give up almost overnight? What role did Western strategy and leadership play in the fall—or was it all due to a correlation of forces? And why did so few experts predict the demise of communism?

In this work, several of the world's leading authorities on communism suggest that a wide range of forces—political, economic, strategic, and religious—along with the indispensable leadership of principled statesmen and brave dissidents, brought about the collapse of communism.

The editor begins by suggesting that when Communists in Eastern and Central Europe admitted they no longer believed in communism, they destroyed the glue of ideology that had maintained their facade of power and authority. Communists also failed, literally, to deliver the goods to the people. They promised bread, but produced food shortages and rationing—except for party members and the *nomenklatura*. And they could not stop the mass media from sustaining and spreading the desire for freedom among the people. Far from being a fortress, Eastern Europe was a Potemkin village easily penetrated by "electronic messages of democracy and capitalism" from the West.

Zbigniew Brzezinski argues that Marxism-Leninism was "an alien doctrine" imposed by an imperial power culturally repugnant to the dominated peoples of Eastern Europe. Disaffection was strongest in the cluster of states with the deepest cultural ties with Western Europe—East Germany, Czechoslovakia, Hungary, and Poland. In Poland, the two key factors were the trade union movement, Solidarity, and the "mighty" Catholic Church.

There were incidental causes of the Soviet Union's dissolution, Richard Pipes states, like the invasion of Afghanistan, the Chernobyl nuclear disaster, and the vacillating personality of Mikhail Gorbachev. And there were more profound levels of causation like economic stagnation, the aspiration of national minorities, and intellectual dissent. But "the decisive catalyst," asserts Pipes, was the utopian and coercive nature of communism's objectives.

During the Stalin years, Robert Conquest points out, there was a huge demographic catastrophe in the Soviet Union with millions of excess deaths. Many who survived lost years of their lives in labor camps, and the whole population was put into a "lasting state of extreme repression." After World War II, communist parties all over Eastern Europe were established "in force and fraud" and followed a Stalinist pattern of intra-party purges, public trials, and mass terror. It has been said that German consciousness took centuries to recover from the Thirty Years' War. It is with such a "massive and profound catastrophe," says Conquest, that the impact of the Stalin period on Russia should be compared.

Marxism, argues Martin Malia, was the decisive factor in the collapse of communism. It was the perverse genius of Marxism to present "an unattainable utopia as an infallibly scientific enterprise." Two often unremarked reasons for the end of communism, Michael Novak writes, were atheism's effect on the soul and economic vitality. Communism set out to destroy the "human capital" on which a free economy and a polity are based and in so doing sowed the seeds of its own destruction.

Soviet economics, Andrzej Brzeski states, was fatally flawed from the beginning. Replacing private property rights with state ownership gave rise to a huge class of functionaries committed only to preserving their domains and pleasing their political bosses. A Soviet cartoon in which a factory's production consisted of one enormous nail, because the factory's bonus was tied to the total weight of output, epitomized the central problem of centralized communist economics. Only the sustained use of force, credible terror, and an artificially maintained sense of isolation, says Brzeski, "could keep the communism system from collapsing."

The cold war, Brian Crozier states, was in fact several wars—a secret espionage war, a military war of nerves emphasizing possible nuclear confrontation, a war of peripheral col-

onization by the Soviet Union in places like Cuba, and a real
war of military invasion, as in Afghanistan. There were two
incidents in 1983 that helped make it clear to Moscow it could
not win the cold war—the U.S. "invasion" of Marxist-held
Grenada and President Reagan's launching of the Strategic Defense Initiative.

Sad to say, concludes Paul Hollander, Western assessments
of communist systems were more often than not mistaken,
"sometimes grotesquely and spectacularly so." The most favorable evaluations of the Soviet Union prevailed during the
early and mid-1930s: the period of the famines, the Great
Purge, the show trials, mass arrests and murders, and the consolidation of the cult of Stalin. Western intellectuals' admiration of communist China peaked during one of the most destructive and bloody chapters of Chinese history—the
Cultural Revolution of the late 1960s. A major conclusion to
be drawn from Western misjudgments of communism, suggests Hollander, is that the attempt to judge "the virtues and
vices of any society" must take into account the extent to
which that society accommodates or frustrates basic human
needs and aspirations.

Political scientist Joshua Maravchik has written that "if
we cannot get straight the rights and wrongs of the struggle
between Communism and anti-Communism, itself perhaps
the greatest moral struggle of this century, then it is hard to
see what other issues we will ever be able to address intelli-
gently."

It is to help set straight the rights and the wrongs, the facts
and the fictions, and the myths and the realities about the
collapse of communism that this work is offered.

1

The Year
of Miracles

Lee Edwards

THE FALL OF COMMUNISM in Eastern and Central Europe in
1989 was produced by decades of political tyranny and economic backwardness. While the West enjoyed remarkable
prosperity and personal freedom, the East fell into an economic and political morass from which no escape seemed possible. With no incentives to compete or modernize, Eastern
Europe's industrial sector became a monument to bureaucratic inefficiency and waste, "a museum of the early industrial age." As the *New York Times* pointed out, Singapore, an
Asian city-state of only two million people, exported 20 percent more machinery to the West in 1987 than all of Eastern
Europe.[1] Life expectancy declined dramatically in the Soviet
bloc, and infant mortality rose during communist rule. The

---

1. "Survey of East European Economies," *New York Times*, December
20, 1987.

only groups exempted from social and economic hardship were Communist Party leaders, upper-echelon military officers, and the managerial elite.

But all the while, the once-impenetrable Iron Curtain was being breached by modern communications and technology, allowing the peoples of Eastern Europe to see how the other half of Europe lived. Increasingly, Poles, Hungarians, Czechs, and East Germans demanded change and reform, not only in the marketplace but in the realm of human rights and liberties. The demands began as early as 1956, when Polish communist leader Wladyslaw Gomulka defied Soviet president Nikita Khrushchev, despite the presence of Soviet tanks, and Hungarian communist leader Imre Nagy was executed after a mass uprising that was brutally crushed by the Soviet army. In 1968, the democratic potential of the "Prague Spring" so frightened Soviet leader Leonid Brezhnev that he ordered the other Warsaw Pact states (except Romania) to join Moscow in invading Czechoslovakia and crushing the new freedoms. Faced with the challenge of Solidarity in 1981, the Polish communist government declared martial law and outlawed the free trade union. Brezhnev considered invading Poland but finally let the Jaruzelski government handle the crisis, making it clear that the Soviet Union would intervene if necessary. For nearly forty years, the communist regimes of Eastern Europe depended on the Soviets to pull their chestnuts out of any fire, but by the mid-1980s, when Mikhail Gorbachev came to power, the Soviet Union could no longer afford to maintain the empire it had so carefully and expensively built.

Even those prescient few who predicted the end of communism ("What I am describing now is . . . the march of freedom and democracy which will leave Marxism-Leninism on the ash heap of history": Ronald Reagan, 1982; "The idea of communism is essentially dead": Zbigniew Brzezinski, 1988) did not anticipate how quickly Marxism-Leninism would collapse in Eastern and Central Europe in the miracle year of 1989.[2] Why did the governments of these Soviet satellites, seemingly secure and in firm control of their populations, fall in less than a year like so many giant dominoes? Only a few months before it came crashing down, East German communist boss Erich Honecker defiantly declared that the Berlin Wall would stand for at least another hundred years.

Part of the answer lies in geography. Although separate and distinct countries, Poland, Hungary, East Germany, Czechoslovakia, and Romania were physically and militarily linked. East Germany and Poland had a common border as did Czechoslovakia and Hungary. Romania was bounded on the north by Czechoslovakia and on the west by Hungary. The five communist countries formed a tight little region, as close as the eastern seaboard states of the United States; a flight from East Berlin to Warsaw was shorter than one from Washington, D.C., to Boston. Even nationalistic differences were blurred; as a result of World War II treaties, several million Germans lived in Poland and Czechoslovakia and Hungarians had settled in Slovakia and Romania. Resentment, frustration, and hope, Brzezinski wrote, were all inevitable in this "cluster of states with the deepest cultural ties with Western Europe."[3] What happened in one country inevitably infected the others, as witness the following chronology of 1989.[4]

2. Zbigniew Brzezinski, *The Grand Failure: The Birth and Death of Communism in the Twentieth Century* (New York: Collier Books, 1989), p. xi; Ronald Reagan, "Address to Members of the British Parliament," Palace of Westminster, June 8, 1982, *Speaking My Mind* (New York: Simon and Schuster, 1989), p. 118.

3. Brzezinski, *Grand Failure*, p. 112.

4. See Bernard Gwertzman and Michael T. Kaufman, eds., *The Collapse of Communism* (New York: Times Books, 1990), and, in particular, Madeleine Albright, "The Glorious Revolutions of 1989," in *The New Democratic*

IDEAS THAT COULD NOT BE SQUELCHED

In February, Vaclav Havel was jailed in Prague for participating in human rights protests, and, after months of strikes,
roundtable talks began in Poland between leaders of the still-
outlawed Solidarity union and the communist government.
Communists had insisted that Solidarity was "a spent force,"
but, as the Polish economy worsened and Gorbachev asserted
that he would no longer honor the Brezhnev Doctrine, they
were required to "reckon with ideas they could not squelch
and men they could not subdue."⁵ In March, seventy-five
thousand people demonstrated in Budapest on the anniversary
of the 1848 revolution, demanding a withdrawal of Soviet
troops and free elections. In April, Solidarity and the Polish
government agreed to the first open elections since World War
II; the union's legal status was restored. In May, the Hungarian
government started to dismantle the Iron Curtain along the
border with Austria; Havel was released from jail after serving
only half his sentence. In June, Solidarity won an overwhelming victory over communist opponents in the Soviet bloc's
first free elections in forty years; the vote swept in ninety-nine
of Solidarity's candidates in the one hundred-seat Senate. Imre
Nagy, who had led the 1956 Hungarian uprising against Soviet
domination, was given a hero's burial in Budapest.

Gorbachev reminded the Council of Europe meeting in
Strasbourg in July that he rejected the Brezhnev Doctrine:
"Any interference in domestic affairs and any attempts to re-
strict the sovereignty of states, both friends and allies or any

---

Frontier: A Country by Country Report on Elections in Central and Eastern
Europe (Washington, D.C.: National Democratic Institute for International
Affairs, 1992), pp. 17–18.
    5. Gwertzman and Kaufman, Collapse of Communism, p. 16.

others, are inadmissable."[6] In August, negotiations between Solidarity and the Communists resulted in the selection of Poland's first noncommunist prime minister, Solidarity official Tadeusz Mazowiecki, since the early postwar years. With summer giving way to fall, people were returning from their vacations, but this year the annual retreat led to massive migrations that "changed governments and altered the political map of the continent."[7]

In September, an East German exodus began when Hungary opened its borders with Austria for more than thirteen thousand Germans, and another seventeen thousand GDR citizens fled via West German embassies in Warsaw and Prague. Meanwhile, the communist leadership and the opposition in Hungary agreed on the institution of a multiparty political system. In October, hundreds of thousands began demonstrating every Monday evening in East Germany, leading to the forced resignation of longtime communist leader Erich Honecker. In November, a tidal wave of East Germans poured across the border when travel restrictions were lifted and the Berlin Wall came tumbling down. Bulgaria's Communist Party chief Todor Zhikov stepped down after thirty-five years of rule as fifty thousand people gathered in Sofia, demanding further reforms. Millions of Czechs and Slovaks walked off their jobs and onto the streets, and the communist government in Czechoslovakia collapsed. It appeared that all the countries except Romania were "leapfrogging each other as they raced to democracy."[8]

Poland was the first Soviet satellite to challenge the Com-

6. Ivo Banc, ed., *Eastern Europe in Revolution* (Ithaca: Cornell University Press, 1992), p. 3.
7. Gwertzman and Kaufman, *Collapse of Communism*, pp. 153–54; Banac, *Eastern Europe in Revolution*, p. 3.
8. Gwertzman and Kaufman, *Collapse of Communism*, p. 300.

munist Party's political power. Hungary was the first to have the party rename itself. Bulgaria was the first to consider eliminating the constitutional guarantees of the party's "leading role." Czechoslovakia was the first to condemn the act that validated the Communist Party's authority—the Warsaw Pact invasion of Czechoslakia in 1968. In December 1989, proposals for free elections were made in Bulgaria and mass demonstrations occurred in the Romanian cities of Timisoara and Bucharest. The year of revolutions ended with the death of Romanian despot Nicolae Ceauşescu and the election of Havel as the president of Czechoslovakia's first noncommunist government since the February 1948 coup engineered by Moscow.

THE ROLE OF IDEOLOGY

Another reason communism in Eastern and Central Europe collapsed like a house of cards is to be found in the essential role of ideology. Millions demonstrated in the streets of Budapest, Leipzig, Prague, and other cities, calling for free elections and a free press, demanding democracy because, the leaders of their governments candidly admitted, "We no longer believe in Marxism-Leninism." Without the glue of ideology, the communist facade of power and authority crumbled and the people's natural desire for freedom, dammed up for more than forty years, burst forth. At the time, Gorbachev was extravagantly praised in the West for his pragmatism in admitting the profound "mistakes" of his predecessors and acknowledging the legitimacy of other social systems, but in so doing he called into question the central concepts of communism: democratic centralism, class struggle, world revolution, party discipline, and even the central role of the Communist Party. The Marxist-Leninist governments of Eastern and Central Europe shook and shuddered with each new political and economic reform attempted by its Big Brother.

Gorbachev never resolved the innate contradictions of using glasnost and perestroika to produce a more perfect socialist world. Three years before the August 1991 putsch in the USSR, Brzezinski wrote that "Gorbachev has unleashed forces that make historical discontinuity more likely than continuity."[9] The Soviet leader preached political liberalization but practiced Leninist one-party rule. He courted Western investment but preserved an archaic command economy. He promised "new thinking" in Soviet foreign policy but continued to send massive amounts of arms and materiel to Cuba, which supported the Sandinistas in Nicaragua and the FMLN in El Salvador. Finally, these contradictions culminated in a crisis that brought about the end of communism in the mother country where it had prevailed for nearly seventy-five years and seemed likely to prevail for years to come.

STAGNANT AND CORRUPT

A further reason for the swift slide of communism into oblivion was, quite literally, its inability to deliver the goods. Gorbachev became the head of "a totally stagnant state dominated by a corrupt totalitarian party."[10] President Reagan pointed out, in his 1982 Westminster address to the British Parliament, that although one-fifth of its population worked in agriculture, the Soviet Union was unable to feed its own people: "Were it not for the . . . tiny private sector tolerated in Soviet agriculture," Reagan said, "the country might be on the

---

9. Brzezinski, *Grand Failure*, p. 243.
10. Ibid., p. 41.

brink of famine."[11] Although occupying a mere 3 percent of the arable land, private farms accounted for nearly one-quarter of Soviet farm output and nearly one-third of meat products and vegetables. Communism fell because it was revealed as a fraud. It promised bread but produced food shortages and rationing. It pledged peace but sacrificed its young men in wars in far-off lands. It guaranteed the peasants land but delivered them into collectives. One of the great economic myths of the cold war was that, under communism, the German Democratic Republic had become, by 1980, the eleventh most prosperous nation in the world, with a per capita income of approximately $5,100 and an annual GNP of $100 billion. But between 1961 and 1984, 176,714 East Germans risked death or imprisonment by escaping illegally from what Honecker liked to call "a paradise" for workers. By 1989 life had become so dreary, the environment so polluted, and the *stasi* (the secret police) so omnipresent that 1.5 million citizens had applied for exit visas and as many as five million people, out of a total population of 16.5 million, would have left East Germany if they could.[12]

MESSAGES OF FREEDOM AND DEMOCRACY

Another reason the Iron Curtain no longer divides Europe is that the mass media sustained and spread the desire for freedom among the peoples of Eastern and Central Europe. East German reformers credit West German television and radio with informing the people how much they were being denied

11. Reagan, *Speaking My Mind*, p. 113.
12. Norman M. Naimark, "'Ich will hier raus': Emigration and the Collapse of the German Democratic Republic," in Banac, *Eastern Europe in Revolution*, pp. 77, 83.

by communist rule. During the difficult decade of the 1980s, Poland's Solidarity union relied heavily on the Voice of America, Radio Free Europe, the BBC, and other Western sources for information and inspiration. Much of Czechoslovakia could receive West German and Austrian television, and as a consequence almost everyone in the country knew that the authority of the East German regime was disintegrating and that the Soviets were doing little to shore it up. The long-suffering, long-oppressed citizens of Bucharest and other Romanian cities learned from foreign radio broadcasts about the popular movements for freedom in the other satellite states and were inspired to move against Ceauşescu. Far from being an impregnable communist fortress, Eastern and Central Europe was a giant Potemkin Village with permeable frontiers that were easily penetrated by electronic messages of democracy and capitalism from the West. The communist mass media also had to compete with the increasing use of videocassette recorders and through them the dissemination of democratic ideas and dissident voices. One 1988 estimate placed the number of VCRs at one million in Poland, 300,000 in Hungary, 150,000 in Czechoslovakia, and 50,000 even in Stalinist Bulgaria.

The fall of communism in Eastern Europe began, appropriately enough, in the first nation to be forced by the Soviet Union to accept communism at the end of World War II. What were the factors that made Poland the first Soviet satellite to renounce its communist regime, establish a democratic opposition, hold partly free parliamentary elections, elect a democratic government, and institute free market reforms? First, Brzezinski points out, Poland's modern history has been defined by its militant opposition to Russian domination. Second, the country's fervent Roman Catholicism set it apart from neighbors and its traditional enemy, reinforcing nationalism and Christian beliefs that were at direct variance with those of communism. The church was critically important because, says Adam Michnik, the Polish poet and dissident, it was the first "to provide definite proof that it was possible to be an independent institution in a totalitarian political environment."

Third, in the 1970s, a new industrial proletariat, imbued with a strong, religious spirit, forged an alliance with an anticommunist, social democratic intelligentsia. Fourth, the communist leadership, having borrowed some $30 billion from the West, squandered almost all of it through ineptitude and corruption, preparing the way for the emergence of a genuine people's movement, *Solidarnosc*, or Solidarity, in the mid-1970s. Solidarity confronted the communist regime on every important front: ideologically through its reliance on religion and emphasis on democracy; organizationally through its nationwide alliance with intellectuals, young people, and especially the Catholic Church.[13] In every one of these areas, the mass media, internal as well as external, had a significant impact.

Among the unique elements that brought an end to communism in the other countries of Eastern and Central Europe were (1) a "benign" form of communism and the dark memory of 1956 in Hungary and (2) a democratic tradition and an eloquent, charismatic leader—Vaclav Havel—in Czechoslovakia. But what of the German Democratic Republic, the hardest of the hard-line communist states? East Germany had no grassroots movement like Solidarity; it was ruled by Stalinist rather

---

13. Brzezinski, *Grand Failure*, pp. 114–17; Adam Michnik, "The Moral and Spiritual Origins of Solidarity," in William M. Brenton and Alan Rinzler, eds., *Without Force or Lies: Voices from the Revolution of Central Europe in 1989–90* (San Francisco: Mercury House, 1990), p. 242.

than Gorbachevist Communists; and, far from having any experience of democracy, it had lived under Nazi and then communist tyranny for nearly sixty years. But it had one thing that the other Soviet satellites did not have: a sister nation, West Germany, that lived in freedom and prosperity. No other member of the Warsaw Pact was as continuously exposed to the indisputable evidence of what democracy and a market economy can provide a people and what Marxism-Leninism cannot as the GDR. The means by which this evidence was transmitted to East Germans in their own language was essentially the West German mass media, especially television.

With the exception of Dresden and part of Saxony (located in the southeastern corner of the GDR), all East Germany could receive West German television, mainly due to the relay antennas located in West Berlin. Out of a total population of 16.5 million, about 13.5 million East Germans could and did receive at least three West German channels: the two national channels, ARD and ZDF, and one of several regional channels. Themselves dedicated propagandists, the East German Communists knew what unrestricted access to West German television could do to minds and wills: "The enemy of the people stands on the roof," Communist Party boss Walter Ulbricht once said of television antennas [14]

For nearly forty years, West German media informed East Germans of the reality of everyday life in the West, promoted daily comparison between two vastly different standards of living, encouraged the notion of German solidarity, and provided an appealing political, economic alternative to the deadening life of the GDR. Some of the West German programming was deliberately aimed at the East, such as the parliamentary

14. Elaine Attias, "Liberation on the Airwaves," *Christian Science Monitor*, February 14, 1991, p. 12.

speeches and debates, but most of the programs were intended for audiences in the FRG. Allowed to operate within a liberal democratic framework, West German media preserved liberty at home and promoted desires for the same liberty behind the Berlin Wall. Without democratic *mediapolitik*, there would have been no bloodless revolution of 1989.

A powerful influence on the course of events in East Germany was the development of a prodemocracy movement halfway around the world. When tanks ran over Chinese students in Tiananmen Square on June 4, 1989, their brutal repression filled television screens around the world but perhaps nowhere with so much effect as in East Germany. Dissident Pastor Tureck remembers the impact of those images from Beijing on his parishioners in Leipzig: "We saw Tiananmen Square here in Leipzig on West German television . . . and it influenced our world. Although people were afraid, they were also filled with hope."[15] Many East Germans gathered in Tureck's and other churches to discuss what the events in China meant for their growing protest movement. Party boss Erich Honecker knew how dangerous the virus of democracy was and ordered East German television not to report the Beijing uprising. But the strategy backfired; West German television enabled East German citizens and leaders to see the inspiring events of Tiananmen Square. When the GDR regime openly supported the bloody crackdown of the Chinese communist leadership, East Germans were deeply angered.[16] Their sense of frustration was increased by the vivid pictures of liberty that continued to fill their television screens: Polish communist leader Jaruzelski standing with Lech Walesa while he made a

15. Tara Sonenshine, "The Revolution Has Been Televised," *Washington Post*, October 2, 1990.
16. Ibid.

Solidarity victory salute; soldiers cutting the barbed wire fence along the Austro-Hungarian border; "freedom trains" in Czechoslovakia carrying jubilant East Germans to the West. Television became a window through which the people of East Germany could witness the revolutionary changes all around them. It gave them information and knowledge with which they could challenge the old ways of looking at the world.

The West German channels ARD and ZDF carried extensive reports about the East German citizens in and around the West German embassies in Budapest, Warsaw, and Prague. They ran dozens of interviews with refugees as well as reports about negotiations allowing East Germans to enter the West. East German families watched television for hours, hoping for a glimpse of a relative or friend risking his life to obtain freedom. When it became clear that the Hungarians were not going to shoot, that refugees were cared for, and that the frontier to Austria was penetrable, people began packing. And when they heard refugees explaining how guides helped them through the fields and forests, how the freedom-seekers bribed frontier guards and fended off dogs, thousands of East Germans closed up their apartments, got in their cars, and set off for Hungary. The September 10 announcement by West German foreign minister Hans-Dietrich Genscher, from the balcony of the West German Embassy in Budapest, that Hungary had officially opened its borders to Austria was a highlight in the collapse of communism in Eastern and Central Europe.

The East German government was mystified as to why so many citizens, especially young people, wanted to leave. *Neues Deutschland*, the official Communist Party organ, insisted that "there is neither persecution, nor war, nor public disaster nor any other life- or existence-threatening criteria [in East Germany]." What *Neues Deutschland* and the communist regime did not understand was that a guaranteed cradleto-grave life in the East was no longer enough. As one newly arrived Leipziger put it on West German television: "If you put a bird in a cage and give it something to eat, it still doesn't feel free." In more than 90 percent of the refugee cases, contrary to the expectations of many Western analysts, the two most frequently mentioned reasons for leaving were (1) general political, not economic, conditions and (2) the lack of political freedom, not consumer goods.[17]

Freedom to emigrate had been the first demand, but now East Germans were taking to their own streets and declaring that they wanted to remain but in a far different kind of country. In East Berlin, Dresden, and particularly Leipzig, calls for reform and democratization were raised more and more loudly by larger and larger crowds, whose gatherings were televised by West German cameras and broadcast back into East Germany. Intellectuals, "Greens," and church-related activists founded the New Forum and petitioned for legal status; the minister of the interior turned it down because of New Forum's "anti-state platform."

Beset on all sides, the communist government desperately tried to retain control. Foreign Minister Oskar Fischer announced that by October 7, 1989, the fortieth anniversary of the GDR and the seventeenth anniversary of party boss Honecker's rule, the world would see a stablized situation in East Germany. All East bloc leaders, including Soviet president Gorbachev, were invited to the ceremonies. Anticipating protests, Honecker publicly ordered security forces to crack down on and even shoot demonstrators if necessary, a command that came to be known as the "China solution," after the massacre

17. Naimark, "'Ich will hier raus,'" pp. 85–86.

in Tiananmen Square, which, as previously noted, the GDR had officially applauded.[18]

THE LEIPZIG DEMONSTRATIONS

The threats did not work. During the first week of October, rallies were held in various cities of the GDR, including Leipzig, where the first of the weekly "Monday demonstrations" took place. People sang "We Shall Overcome" and the "Internationale" and shouted slogans like "Legalize New Forum," "We Are Staying Here," and "Gorbi Gorbi," reflecting the socialist rather than liberal democratic inclinations of the participants. The Leipzig demonstrations became the bellwether for the growing sense of community and power that GDR citizens shared in mass meetings throughout the country. The most critical point of the revolution came on October 7, when Gorbachev spoke in East Berlin. Although the Soviet leader only implicitly encouraged reform and reiterated his adherence to the principle of noninterference, he was greeted by chants of "Gorbi, Help Us" and "Glasnost and Perestroika." The appeal to the Soviet model of liberalization was telling as the GDR had long bound itself, economically, militarily, and ideologically, to Moscow. The regime had tried to distance itself from Gorbachev's reforms—Honecker's chief ideologist claimed that each socialist country should build its own type of socialism—but the East German government merely succeeded in isolating itself from its own people and the reformers in other Warsaw Pact countries. Now, with Gorbachev by his side, Honecker still made no concessions in his hard-line address, concluding with the worn-out slogans "Work Together, Plan To-

18. Ibid., p. 88; John Bornemann, *After the Wall: East Meets West in the New Berlin* (New York: Basic Books, 1991), p. 21.

gether, Govern Together" and "Always Forward—Never Back." Gorbachev warned Honecker that "life punishes those who come too late," but the East German leader did not listen or understand the revolutionary fervor that was sweeping the country.[19]

Falling back on traditional Leninist methods, the GDR government unleashed the *volkspolizei* and the *stasi*, who cracked down viciously on demonstrators, particularly in East Berlin. Those arrested were subjected to hours of neo-Nazi interrogations that included being made to stand for hours, legs spread apart, half-naked, in unheated rooms. Incensed citizens called for an immediate investigation. Although the head of the secret police insisted that the demonstrators had provoked the police to violence, the *stasi*'s own videos revealed a different story; one man was sentenced to a six-month imprisonment for calling out "No Violence" about fifteen times. Through word of mouth and Western television, the extent of police brutality became widely known, and the credibility of a regime willing to "inflict such savagery on its citizens with the left hand, while anointing and garlanding itself with the right," was irreparably lost.[20]

Despite the police brutality in Berlin, fifty thousand determined demonstrators, led by students and church activists, took to the streets of Leipzig on Monday, October 9, in a decisive test of the regime's will. Leipzig emerged as the center of the opposition because it was a university town, it had a large network of churches, and the *stasi* were not as well organized there as in East Berlin. Not since June 1953, when the angry

19. Naimark, "'Ich will hier raus,'" pp. 89–90; Bornemann, *After the Wall*, p. 22; German Information Center, *Focus on the German Unification Process* (New York: German Information Center, 1990), p. 1.
20. Bornemann, *After the Wall*, pp. 23–24.

protests of East Berlin workers forced the Communists to bring in Soviet troops to suppress the riots, had there been so great a display of "people power" in East Germany. An unyielding Honecker gave written instructions to the *stasi* to fire on the crowd, à la Tiananmen Square, if necessary.

Late in the afternoon the secret police were waiting for the final attack order, when leaders of the march, including world-renowned conductor Kurt Masur, issued an appeal to both sides to "act with prudence so that a peaceful dialogue will be possible." The demonstrators slowly disbanded, and the security forces did not attack, undoubtedly swayed by the size of the crowd, the moral commitment of the people to nonviolence, and the solemn appeal of Masur and the other march leaders. There was also a more practical reason: Egon Krenz, the Politboro member in charge of security, flew to Leipzig that same day and personally canceled Honecker's order, allowing the protesters to march unmolested.

An uncertain party leadership debated how to respond to the demonstrators. Using their central propaganda instrument, the television program *Aktuelle Kamera*, they issued an appeal for socialist solidarity and resistance to the "evil imperialists" in West Germany. They indicated their willingness to engage in a dialogue, welcomed any suggestions on how to build a more attractive socialism, and, most significantly of all, issued no warnings about further demonstrations. Clearly and publicly, the oppressor's will had been broken.[21] The reformers realized that disciplined, peaceful demonstrations in front of TV cameras were their most powerful weapon.

---

21. Ibid., pp. 25–26; "How the Wall Was Cracked—a Special Report: Party Coup Turned East German Tide," based on reporting by Craig R. Whitney, David Binder, and Serge Schmemann, *New York Times*, November 17, 1990; Gwertzman and Kaufman, *Collapse of Communism*, p. 216.

THE COMMUNISTS: TOO LITTLE, TOO LATE

The Monday night demonstrations in Leipzig grew exponentially: October 9, 70,000; October 16, 120,000; October 23, 300,000; October 30, half a million. Protesters carried posters proclaiming "Stasi Out" and "Legalize New Forum." During the fortieth anniversary celebration, the regime had flooded the stores with bananas, rarely available before. One popular banner now read "Don't Fill Our Mouth with Talk of Reform and Try to Shut Us Up with Bananas." On October 18, the communist government tried to shore up its rapidly fading authority by ousting Honecker as party chief, head of state, and chairman of the Defense Council and dismissing two other hard-line members of the Politboro. Krenz was named the new party leader, but the protests only grew larger, assisted by the regime's placating decision to allow live coverage on East German television and radio. Every reform that the government offered to the people only increased their appetite for more reforms, especially the most important of all, an end to communism.

On November 1, Krenz tried a Gorbachev gambit, flying to Moscow to meet the Soviet president and endorse a version of perestroika—economic and social restructuring—for East Germany. Huge crowds marched in Leipzig, East Berlin, Dresden, and other cities while thousands of East Germans resumed their efforts to get into the West German Embassy in Prague. Finally, on November 4, Krenz announced that citizens of the GDR who wanted to settle in the FRG could travel freely through Czechoslovakia. That same day, more than half a million and perhaps as many as one million people demonstrated for democracy in the heart of East Berlin, the largest crowd East Germany had ever seen. At the four-hour rally, Gunter Schabowski, the East Berlin Communist Party chief, tried to strike a note of reconciliation, conceding that "bitter things have been said . . . but only if we speak to each other can we create a new East Germany." The crowd's response was short and to the point: "Shut up!" Among the last speakers was a popular actress, Steffie Spira, who concluded her brief remarks by saying: "I want the Government to do what I am about to do. Step down."[22] The government got the message—three days later, the Council of Ministers resigned and called on Parliament to choose a new government; the next day, the Politboro quit. The death rattle of the GDR could now be heard by everyone.

The final action—bringing down the Berlin Wall—came on Thursday evening, November 9, when Schabowski gave a briefing to reporters that was carried live on both East and West German television. The communist official announced a new travel law under which East Germans could leave the GDR directly without going through a third country. A journalist immediately asked if the new law also extended to the West Berlin border? A pause and then came the answer, "Yes." Did the new law mean that any GDR citizen could, without a legal passport, travel across the border into West Berlin? Could Germans divided by forty years meet and talk again? Again the answer came, "Yes." Within minutes, hundreds and then thousands of East Berliners were lined up at border crossings.

On the other side, Western television and radio crews waited to record their crossing and capture history. Commanding officers of the border guards, noticing the Western television, overwhelmed by the mobs, unwilling to implement a "Chinese solution," and aware that the world had changed radically in the last month, gave way and opened the gates.

22. Serge Schmemann, "500,000 in East Berlin Rally for Change; Emigres Are Given Passage to West," *New York Times*, November 4, 1989; Gwertzman and Kaufman, *Collapse of Communism*, pp. 171–74; Bornemann, *After the Fall*, pp. 28–29; Naimark, "'Ich will hier raus,'" pp. 90–91.

After twenty-eight years, two months, twenty-seven days, and the deaths of eighty who tried to cross it, the wall was no more. Western stations broke into their regular programming to announce the opening of the wall, bringing tens of thousands of West and East Berliners into the streets for an ecstatic reunion. Western television continued its live coverage throughout the night, helping to create a New Year's Eve atmosphere. Over the weekend, two million people visited the West, bought chocolates, fruit, and souvenirs, and then returned home to a country that would never be the same again. Indeed, it would cease to be a country in less than eleven months.[23]

The nearly bloodless revolution of East Germany resulted from the convergence of several factors: (1) the impact of liberating events in neighboring countries, especially the emergence of Solidarity in Poland and Hungary's measured moves toward democratization; (2) Gorbachev's consistent rejection of the Brezhnev Doctrine and his pursuit of glasnost and perestroika in the Soviet Union and other communist states; (3) the never-abandoned desire of Germans for German solidarity; (4) the emergence of a human rights movement and other reform groups like the Greens; (5) the courageous stand of the Evangelical (Lutheran) Church; and (6) the unwillingness of the communist leadership to use massive force against the people to maintain Marxism-Leninism. The mass media, especially those of West Germany, played a critical part, sometimes encouraging action, sometimes discouraging action, but always contributing to a powerful democratic *mediapolitik* that tore gaping holes in the Iron Curtain and brought down a concrete wall that many thought would stand for decades to come.

23. Bornemann, *After the Fall*, pp. 1–3; Gwertzman and Kaufman, *Collapse of Communism*, p. 222.

2

The
Grand Failure

Zbigniew Brzezinski

A SINGLE CRUCIAL FACT is the key to understanding the fall of communism in Eastern Europe: Marxism-Leninism was an alien doctrine imposed on the region by an imperial power whose rule was culturally repugnant to the dominated peoples. As a result, a process of organic rejection of communism by East European societies a phenomenon similar to the human body's rejection of a transplanted organ—ensued. This process played out in a contest between national forces seeking ways to free their societies from Moscow's dogma and Soviet attempts to develop new ways to retain ultimate control over the region's destiny.

Although Marxism was first conceived in Western Europe, its adaptation to Russia's oriental despotic political culture

This chapter has been adapted from the author's *The Grand Failure* (New York: Collier Books, 1989).

brutalized its initially humanistic orientation. When Stalin forcibly grafted Soviet-style communism on the countries of Eastern Europe, he transplanted Marxism-Leninism-Stalinism to societies that identified themselves largely with Western Europe's cultural, religious, and intellectual heritage. As a result, the Soviet empire in Eastern Europe is unique in imperial history in that the dominant nation was not viewed by the subject people as culturally superior.

For a while, however, communist ideology managed to compensate for that condition. Even though most East Europeans viewed Russian domination as a cultural setback, many believed the communist doctrine had the potential for more rapid modernization and industrialization. Since the Soviet Union was at the time considered to be the model of communism in practice, ideology served to justify not only imitation of the Soviet Union but acceptance—as a positive historical necessity—of domination by the Kremlin.

Thus, the failure of the Soviet model had devastating consequences for the Soviet imperial domain. It accelerated the attrition of the communist doctrine as the empire's unifying bond. It also intensified resentment against an external domination, increasingly viewed as the source of the region's growing social and cultural retardation. It imposed on Moscow the need to buttress the empire by new ties. These, in turn, stimulated additional national hostility against the Kremlin's central control.

As a result, two conflicting pulls strained the fabric of the Soviet empire in Eastern Europe. On the one hand, a process of self-emancipation from Soviet ideological control threatened to dilute—or even break—the imperial bonds. On the other hand, Soviet-sponsored efforts to intensify military-economic integration sought to counter these centrifugal dynamics. The first thus involved organic rejection of communism

by much of Eastern Europe. The second entailed efforts to enhance Eastern Europe's dependence for its territorial security
on the goodwill and decisions of the Kremlin.

IDEOLOGICAL TRANSPLANTATION
AND TRANSMUTATION

Czeslaw Milosz, in his celebrated book *The Captive Mind*,
conveyed dramatically how initially gripping was the hold of
Marxist-Leninist doctrine even on noncommunist East Europeans, crushed by Hitler and then "liberated" by Stalin. A
sense of irresistible power radiated from the Stalinist regime.
At the same time, the democratic West conveyed a sense of
indifference to the fate of Eastern Europe. Combined with the
monumental scope of the social experiment undertaken in the
Soviet Union, that doctrine cumulatively created a sense of
historical inevitability to the sovietization of the region. Destiny seemed to dictate a posture of acceptance and even of
conversion.

Fervent fanaticism among the true believers—the newly
established communist power elite—was at an even higher
pitch. They saw themselves as riding the crest of history. An
ecstatic exclamation to the Central Committee of the ruling
Polish party in July 1948 by one of its most fervently Stalinist
leaders, Mieczyslaw Moczar, captured perfectly the prevailing
mood among the disciplined faithful: "For us, partymen, the
Soviet Union is our Motherland, and our frontiers today I cannot define, today beyond Berlin, and tomorrow at Gibraltar."

Moreover, there were admittedly some positive tangibles
for the region in the initial communist transformation. It was
thus not all a matter of abstract ideological attraction. Eastern
Europe emerged from the war devastated and acutely conscious of its relative lag in comparison with both the indus-

trially more advanced Western Europe and the newly industrialized Stalinist Russia. The Soviet-imposed communist elites
made it their central goal to combine desirable social reforms,
particularly the much-needed redistribution of land to the
peasants, with rapid industrialization. They set the goal of
matching within two decades and then surpassing in heavy
industrial production the more advanced West European economies. In fact, rapid rates of industrial growth during the initial period were for a while achieved.

The first decade of communist rule in Eastern Europe was
also the time of rapid social promotion for the socially disad-
vantaged. This was especially so in the less advanced countries, such as Romania and Bulgaria, but also to a lesser extent
in Poland and Hungary. All had large numbers of rural poor, as
well as some highly radicalized industrial workers who were
willing and even eager to identify with the new regime. For
them, the onset of communist rule opened the doors to rapid
advancement through greater educational opportunities, as
well as in the institutions of power, notably, the police and
military. To a lesser extent, that was also true of Czechoslovakia and East Germany, although in these countries the industrial working class provided the more plentiful source of
recruitment for the revolutionary regime.

In the initial period of communist construction, the new
rulers were able to also exploit the enthusiasm of some seg-
ments of the intellectual community who were captivated by
a notion of state-sponsored social engineering and the pseudo-
scientific vision of communism. In the early years, the new
order also mobilized support from many of the young, who
were drawn by the vision of a new age, by grandiose urban and
industrial projects, and by the humanitarian goals of social
reform. The notion of building a new and just social order on
the ruins of the past was genuinely appealing to those trau-

matized by World War II and seeking some firm but idealistic sense of historical direction.

Although highly dependent on Soviet power, the new East European communist regimes were not without some genuine social backing. As a broad generalization, it may be said that communism initially enjoyed the most domestic support in Czechoslovakia and in Bulgaria and the least in Poland. In Czechoslovakia and Bulgaria, strong communist movements existed even before the advent of Soviet military power, along with considerable traditional affinity for the Russians. In Poland, national resistance to sovietization was strong and persistent.

Although the Communists enjoyed some support, nowhere did they have majority support. In fact, during the initial phase the new rulers were preoccupied with crushing and altogether eliminating any domestic political alternative. The concept of the class struggle, reinforced by Stalin's "dialectical" doctrine—that the struggle actually intensifies with growing success in the building of socialism—was used to justify the prolonged application of Stalinist-type terror throughout the region. Particularly violent were the years 1948–53, during which Eastern Europe was subjected to intense sovietization. The communist regimes executed tens of thousands, imprisoned hundreds of thousands, staged show trials, and practiced mass intimidation.

Without dwelling at length on the immeasurable human suffering, a few statistics help convey the scale of the terror involved in the sovietization of Eastern Europe. In Hungary, with a population at the time of six million, between 1950 and 1953 some 387,000 alleged political opponents—or more than 5 percent of Hungarians—were imprisoned, according to the careful accounting provided by Paul Lendvai in *Das Eigenwillige Ungarn* (1987). Following the suppression of the Hungarian uprising in 1956, the Soviet-installed Kádár regime executed an estimated two thousand to four thousand political opponents. During the "Prague Spring" of 1968, the communist regime initiated an examination of its past, thereby surfacing some staggering statistics: In 1951, in the relatively compliant Czechoslovakia, more than 100,000 people (including more than 6,100 priests, monks, and nuns) were incarcerated in concentration camps, while bloody inner-party purges resulted in the execution of 278 of the party's own top leaders. In Poland, the crushing of the armed resistance to communist rule resulted in about forty-five thousand deaths, followed by an estimated five thousand executions of various political opponents. To that must be added an unknown number—but certainly in the tens of thousands—who were deported to Soviet concentration camps and who never returned.

Through this massive and organized violence, the communist leaders succeeded in imposing the Soviet-type totalitarian system on Eastern Europe. They crushed the existing societies and thereby made possible the creation of a new social and political order. But it would be a mistake to see the defining characteristics of the mundane day-to-day realities of life under a totalitarian system in organized terror. Intense and widespread terror was used both as a means of social reconstruction and as the ultimate tool of perpetuating the system, but, once established, that system became characterized, above all, by pervasive and petty bureaucratization of all aspects of normal life. This was the case to a degree and in a manner that a superficial observer from the pluralistic and democratic West could not comprehend.

The infliction of the Soviet-type system on Eastern Europe gave rise to a new ruling class, one that owed everything to communism in general and Soviet power in particular. Moreover, the less social support this class enjoyed, the more it tended to identify itself with the Soviet Union, its sponsor and protector. Moscow could count on the fealty, indeed servility, of those who directly depended on the Kremlin for their own survival. Self-interest as well as ideology thus created a tight bond of loyalty and dependence, with Stalin deified at the apex of a disciplined pyramid of power.

But the apparent external cohesion of the Soviet bloc obscured the underlying internal fragility of the new regimes. That fragility surfaced shortly after Stalin' death in 1953. Thus by the early 1950s, the luster of the mirage of Marxism-Leninism's grand oversimplification was already beginning to dissolve in the face of harsh realities. The limited initial enthusiasm for communism had largely faded as the creeping awareness of Western Europe's more rapid recovery bred disillusionment and resentments. Moreover, the abrupt disappearance of Stalin deprived the Soviet leadership of a towering and intimidating personality.

As soon as political splits developed within the Kremlin leadership, and as soon as Soviet leaders began to tamper with the Stalinist legacy, crises mushroomed in Eastern Europe. The resulting upheaval in East Germany in 1953, followed by massive political instability in Poland and by large-scale violence in Hungary in 1956, would certainly have caused the collapse of communism in all of Eastern Europe, had it not been for the direct Soviet military intervention. Even in a country initially as well predisposed toward Moscow as Czechoslovakia, the experience with the Soviet-style system proved to be totally disillusioning. The Prague Spring of 1968, which was also crushed by Soviet arms, demonstrated the persistent unwillingness of the people to accept as permanent a political and socioeconomic system so explicitly derived from an alien tradition. The Soviet military occupation in turn further dramatized the condition of continued dependence and the status as puppets of the East European communist regimes.

Not surprisingly, disaffection tended to be strongest in the cluster of states with the deepest cultural ties with Western Europe: East Germany, Czechoslovakia, Hungary, and Poland. For them, sovietization meant a profound break with both their political and their cultural past. For a while, even history and tradition can be suppressed and driven from the surface of social life. A geopolitical doctrine based on domination through overwhelming power, such as the Brezhnev Doctrine, can define the outer limits of dissent, creating the illusion of stability and even prompting the outward appearance of resignation. For a while, also, cultural life can assume external forms of doctrinal obeisance and even national aspirations can be muted. Underneath it all, however, resentment, frustration, and hope continue to ferment, waiting for an opportunity to assert themselves again.

The successful Soviet military interventions taught the East Europeans that a direct challenge to Soviet preeminence and to their communist systems would not work. The West would not help them. Their frightened communist elites would appeal for Soviet help, and the imperial Soviet rulers would use force to prevail. Hence, more indirect and more patient methods would have to be applied. The transformation would have to come from within, take essentially peaceful forms, and occur gradually. In a sense, a strategy of historical stealth would have to involve the co-optation of at least a portion of the ruling class and entail some informal coordination with proponents of change in adjoining East European countries. It would also have to take advantage of propitious splits within the Soviet leadership.

Moscow's determination to use arms, if necessary, to keep communism in power in Eastern Europe had a further, unexpected effect: It obviously reassured even the weakest communist elites, such as the one in Poland, that the Kremlin would not permit their resentful peoples to rise successfully against them. That, quite naturally, served to enhance the sense of personal and political security of the native Communists. At the same time, the enhancement of the elite's security had the paradoxical effect of narrowing the gap between such elites and their peoples. By fostering an enforced sense of shared destiny between the rulers and the ruled, these elites became more susceptible to the appeal of deeply felt national aspirations. By becoming more entrenched politically, and by feeling more confident historically, the communist ruling class gradually became less servile nationally.

Furthermore, the Stalinist period was too short to replow totally the East European societies, to erase their sense of cultural and national identity, or to destroy their specific political traditions. With time, but in varying degrees, a sense of distinctiveness increasingly surfaced—to the detriment of Soviet control. In East Germany, it focused on the increased pursuit of closer human contacts with the rest of Germany. In Romania, it involved the emergence of a rabidly nationalist and highly personal dictatorship reminiscent in many ways of the prewar Romanian fascist Iron Guard. In Hungary, it focused on the energetic effort to promote a more decentralized economic system and on a quiet opening of social-cultural contacts with neighboring Austria. Even in superloyal Bulgaria, it assumed the form of an ambitious program to carve out a distinctive and highly specialized economic role. Only in dispirited Czechoslovakia, following the Soviet occupation of 1968, did quiet resignation seem to prevail throughout the Brezhnev years.

POLISH SELF-EMANCIPATION

The biggest change and the greatest challenge both to continued Soviet control and to the distinctive trademarks of the Soviet-type system took place, not surprisingly, in Poland. It was, after all, the largest and ethnically the most homogeneous of the Soviet-dominated East European states. Its modern history has been defined largely in terms of opposition to Russian domination. Its Roman Catholic religion, which sets Poland apart from its immediate neighbors and traditional enemies, served to reinforce the sense of nationalism and imbue it with a doctrinal content directly at variance with communism. Almost everything in Polish society and in Polish history conspired against a communist system imposed on Warsaw from Moscow.

The word *conspired* is not a mere literary flourish. It describes accurately the Polish posture toward the prevailing communist system in Poland and toward the unequal relationship imposed by Russia. The 125-year-long subjugation of Poland by its neighbors deeply ingrained the tradition of conspiratorial resistance into the national psyche. To resist repeated partitions and preserve their national identity, the Poles had to learn to practice an internalized national life, quietly conspiring among themselves to evade the often brutal attempts to stamp out all signs of national consciousness. The fact that during the nineteenth century the Russians applied the most severe repressions conditioned the Poles for a more sustained resistance in the twentieth century—to a doctrine not only alien to their traditions and religion but forcibly grafted on their society by these very same Russians.

The enduring strength of the national sentiment enabled Poland to preserve some important islands of national autonomy and authenticity throughout the Stalinist era. The Roman Catholic Church was the most important. Some intellectual autonomy was also preserved, though to a much more limited extent. After 1956, the peasantry was freed from the oppressive efforts to impose Soviet-style collectivization on Polish agriculture. The scope of political and doctrinal control over the society by the state was thus significantly reduced.

The spontaneous social effort to inculcate the young with the history of the Polish underground resistance during World War II to both the Nazi and the Soviet invaders played an important role as well. The more the communist regime maligned that resistance, the more attractive its traditions and sacrifices became to the younger postwar generation. This helped sustain large pockets of passive and quiet conspiratorial resistance to spiritual communization. That passive resistance kept open the option of reaching out someday for more ambitious societal self-emancipation.

That day dawned in the 1970s. By then the disenchantment with the existing system had become pervasive. Even the social strata originally sympathetic to some of the communist-sponsored social reforms had come to view both the Soviet Union and the regime in Poland as brakes on social progress. The intellectuals were thoroughly disaffected and totally reoriented toward the West. The ambition of every aspiring scholar was to spend some time in the West, with the Soviet Union viewed as a provincial backwater. American-sponsored cultural and academic exchanges, notably those developed over a number of years by the Ford Foundation, had a major impact, undoing two decades of regime-sponsored efforts to link Polish culture with that of its eastern neighbor. Polish youth had long forgotten its initial (and, in any case, quite partial and brief) infatuation with the notion of building a new society and was acutely aware of and attracted by the West's new lifestyle, technological progress, and cultural experimentation. The emancipated peasantry was almost totally Catholic and traditional in its outlook.

The biggest change in political attitude occurred in the industrial working class. Although numerically weak in prewar agrarian Poland, it had a rich syndicalist tradition and was generally of a socialist orientation. The Polish Socialist Party (PPS) had been in the forefront of the struggle for Poland's national rebirth and had played a major role in the World War II underground. After the war the Communists crushed the party, and its remnants were amalgamated into the new ruling party, totally dominated by Moscow's Communists. That ruling party then effected the postwar industrialization of the country, creating thereby a new postpeasant first-generation industrial class more susceptible to communist ideological and organizational mobilization. It is noteworthy, for example, that the 1956 workers' rebellion in Poznan, which precipitated the emergence in Warsaw of a less servile communist regime under Wladyslaw Gomulka, was undertaken by the older, more traditional, and more politically aware workers but with less resonance among the new first-generation industrial proletariat.

These social currents gained a symbolically important spearhead through the appearance of a genuinely charismatic worker-leader, Lech Wałesa. His personal history and political maturation were a microcosm of these broader trends. Born in a peasant family, brought up in a deeply religious environment, turned into a dockyard worker in Gdansk through Poland's postwar industrialization, disaffected by the continued poverty of the urban proletariat, converted to anticommunism by the privileges and abuse of power by the self-centered party officialdom, politicized by the bloody confrontation between the dockyard workers and the police in the early 1970s, and eventually assisted by a group of intellectual political activists, Wałesa became the leader and the symbol of the movement that galvanized Poland and gained worldwide recognition.

The name of that movement, *Solidarnosc*, or Solidarity, also took on great symbolic importance. The essence of totalitarian rule is the elimination of any autonomous political life and the automization of society. The objective is to make certain that every individual is left alone to face the system as a whole, feeling isolated and often adrift in his or her internal but never publicly expressed opposition. Solidarity conveyed the very opposite message. It signaled a new reality of shared consciousness, of collective confidence, and of an alliance between different social strata or classes. It confronted the communist regime on a broad front: ideologically through its reliance on religion and through its emphasis on democracy and intense commitment to patriotism; organizationally through its nationwide structure and through its alliance with the intellectuals, the young, and, especially, the church.

Solidarity also capitalized on the tangible failures of the communist system. The country's communist leaders, having borrowed during the early 1970s some $30 billion from the West, simply squandered, through ineptitude and corruption, that massive injection of capital that could have been used to revitalize the economy. The resulting economic crisis necessitated the austerity measures that not only sparked worker unrest but also destroyed any lingering social respect for the country's communist rulers. Communism no longer represented social advancement for any major social class.

The peasants despised the regime because of the bitter encounter with collectivization and hence did not even credit it for the land reform of the mid-1940s. The urban masses suffered acutely under continuing housing shortages, poor services, endless queuing even for the simplest essentials of life, and escalating food costs. Even the educational system—long a point of special pride on the part of the Communists, who liked to contrast it with the situation in prewar Poland—no longer served as a source of social promotion.

The shared consciousness of deprivation and politicization and a sense of wider social solidarity could not be destroyed even by the imposition of martial law in December 1981. By then a new national consciousness had been forged, one that integrated into the outlook of the masses the very traditions and even historical memories that the Soviet-sponsored regime had for thirty years strived to eradicate. The restoration of the authentic national personality became the enduring legacy of the more promising period of Solidarity's open existence, and it had the effect of transforming Poland's political landscape.

Solidarity thus precipitated the spiritual self-emancipation of the country, even though the preexisting political framework continued because of martial law. Nonetheless, the political framework, despite formal institutional continuity, was henceforth filled with a different substance. Martial law was able to destroy and suppress the surface organizational aspects of Solidarity, but it could not prevent the emergence of a de facto alternative political elite and the associated rebirth of genuine political life in Poland—even if that new life still operated partially below the official surface.

3

The Fall of
the Soviet Union

Richard Pipes

THE FALL OF the Soviet Union is a momentous subject. In less than a decade since that event happened, a vast literature has emerged and no doubt an even larger flood will follow. For indeed, the event was unique in history. All empires have come to an end sooner or later but almost always as the result of long decay culminating in military defeat. The decline and fall of the Roman Empire took at least two centuries, and even after its collapse, its successor state in the East, Byzantium, survived for another thousand years. The tsarist empire lasted for more than four and a half centuries; its agony, accompanied by a succession of military debacles and the emergence of an aggressive revolutionary movement, spanned half a century. But the Soviet Union disintegrated at the seeming peak of its world influence, without a shot being fired, almost instantaneously.

No wonder, therefore, that the causes of this occurrence

have intrigued many minds, the more so that hardly anyone had foreseen it; the consensus of expert opinion held that the Soviet Union was here to stay, a stable regime capable of coping with any challenges. This perception provided the theoretical underpinning of the policy of detente; like it or not, we were told, we must accommodate ourselves as best we can to the existence of the USSR and its bloc.

Before proceeding to discuss the various explanations of the Soviet collapse, a few words need be said about the problem of historical "causes." Probably no issue is harder for the historian to deal with because causes operate on disparate levels: there are incidental causes, there are substantive causes, and there are long-term causes, in each of which human will plays a progressively diminishing role.

Let us take, for example, the causes of World War I. It is common knowledge that the event that precipitated the war was the assassination, on June 28, 1914, of Grand Duke Francis Ferdinand of Austria by a Balkan terrorist. The murder could have remained a regrettable but isolated episode in turbulent Balkan history were it not for Austria's decision to declare war on Serbia followed by the order of Nicholas II for a general mobilization of Russian forces. This order, in turn, induced Germany to declare war on Russia and its ally, France. Such events constituted, as it were, a secondary level of causation. But the profoundest cause of the war was certainly the old rivalry for European hegemony between Germany, on the one hand, and Britain and France, on the other.

What then "caused" World War I? All these factors. But decisive in my judgment was the last because, given the geopolitical competition between the two great power blocs, sooner or later a pretext for the outbreak of hostilities would have been found.

Similar considerations apply to the Russian Revolution of

1917. The immediate precipitating event was the mutiny of the Petrograd garrison in late February of that year. Generals, worried lest the mutiny spread to the front, urged the tsar to abdicate in favor of his son. When, inspired by patriotism, Nicholas followed their advice, the country plunged into anarchy. In fact, a mutiny on a much grander scale, affecting front-line troops, broke out in France soon afterward. Yet because French society and government were cohesive, as those Russian were not, the mutiny was contained without any damage to the political system or to the pursuit of the war.

Much the same holds true of the theme of this discussion. As one surveys the secondary literature, one finds each author focusing on a particular cause as decisive for the outcome: some stress incidental factors, others substantive ones, and others yet systemic ones, embedded in the nature of the Soviet regime.

Among the incidental factors, three stand out: Afghanistan, Chernobyl, and Mikhail Gorbachev.

Thus one observer, Anthony Arnold, argues that the Soviet defeat in Afghanistan was a major cause of the union's collapse because it undermined public support for aggressive foreign policies, inhibiting Moscow from resorting to military force to crush the so-called counterrevolution in Poland, which facilitated the unraveling of its East European empire. Afghanistan was the "pebble" on which the USSR stumbled.[1]

The explosion of a nuclear reactor at Chernobyl in April 1986 undermined the authority of the government not so much because it revealed the inadequate safety of Soviet reactors but because the government, even though committed to glasnost', lied about it. It took *Pravda* ten days to report the

1. Anthony Arnold, *The Fateful Pebble: Afghanistan's Role in the Fall of the Soviet Union* (Novato, Calif., 1992).

disaster, and then it did so only because it could no longer prevaricate—the disaster had become widely known from foreign broadcasts. That delay cost many lives because it slowed down evacuation efforts and thus brought discredit on the government.

The intervention in Afghanistan and the Chernobyl incident are excellent examples of incidental causes—the kind that can trigger a chain of catastrophic events but only if the body politic is already unwell. There can be little doubt that both could have been checked had the Soviet Union been as sound as the majority of experts claimed it was. After all, the far more costly and contentious U.S. intervention in Vietnam did not bring down the U.S. government or even inflict lasting damage on it.

A third example of an incidental cause is the personality of Mikhail Gorbachev. Chosen to head the party and the state after a succession of decrepit leaders, he was expected to infuse fresh blood into an anemic regime without changing its essential features. But Gorbachev turned out to be a weak, vacillating politician, unable to decide between progress and stability. In the end, against his own wishes, he eviscerated the system that still had some life left in it.

When we turn to the next, more-profound level of causation, we confront factors that, although not immune to manipulation, were more difficult to cope with because they were either embedded in the system or lay outside the rulers' control. Resolving them, where possible, could only have been accomplished by tampering with the system, which carried obvious risks. Among these, three stand out: economic stagnation; the aspirations of the national minorities; and intellectual dissent.

That the Soviet economy in the 1980s was in deep trouble was a matter of common knowledge. The CIA forecast virtually zero growth, and even within the Soviet Union voices were heard calling for major changes in the way the economy was run. A heavy and unanticipated blow was the sudden drop in the price of petroleum, the country's leading export commodity and the prime earner of hard currency; the decline in earnings from this source forced Moscow to resort to heavy borrowing abroad. Attempts to liberalize and rationalize the way the economy operated encountered staunch resistance from the bureaucracy, whose livelihood depended on its perquisites; introducing rational calculations into economic management presented a lethal threat to its interests. The bureaucracy's defiance, passive and active, impelled Gorbachev to seek popular support by introducing representative institutions. This had the effect of destroying the party's monopoly on political power—the essential feature of the regime instituted by Lenin—and soon brought the whole edifice down.

Forged during and immediately after the Civil War, the Soviet Union was an empire in the fullest sense of the word, even if, in contrast to European empires whose colonies lay overseas, its territory was contiguous to the metropolis. It was expanded after World War II to include most of Eastern Europe. In contrast to Western empires, which subjected to colonial rule exclusively non-Europeans, the Russian empire subjugated also European nations. It should be obvious that in an age when all other empires had been broken up, either voluntarily or by force, the Russian empire could not last; history was not likely to make it a unique exception to the worldwide process of decolonization.

But the Soviet authorities preferred to ignore this reality, pretending that they were not an empire but another "melting pot" in which diverse ethnic groups dissolved their ethnic identity in a common "Soviet" nationality. Of course, this was fiction if only because, unlike the United States, whose popu-

lation consisted overwhelmingly of immigrants, the Soviet
Union's inhabitants occupied their historic homelands. Let-
ting go of the empire was for the Russians exceedingly difficult
because their nation-state had grown up concurrently with the
empire to the point where the two became indistinguishable.
Furthermore, they had traditionally compensated for their
poverty and backwardness with the proud awareness that they
had the largest state in the world.

So they did nothing and things soon got out of hand. The
instant the politicians of the non-Russian republics sensed the
center wobbling, they began to clamor for national rights.
Georgia, Lithuania, and Estonia declared their independence
in March 1991; Latvia, in May; Russia, Uzbekistan, and Mol-
dova, in June. The Ukraine, the largest and most populous of
the non-Russian republics, and Belorussia declared themselves
sovereign states in July 1991, a decision that was ratified on
December 1 by more than 90 percent of the Ukraine's population. Gorbachev made a desperate attempt to preserve the
Union by drafting a new constitutional charter that would
have maintained the substance of the old imperial arrange-
ment while making some formal concessions to the subject
nations, but he was overtaken by events. The formal dissolution of the USSR took place in December 1991 as a result of an
agreement among the heads of state of Russia, Belorussia, and
the Ukraine. So in the literal sense the collapse of the Soviet
Union was directly caused by the nationalities.[2]

But then where are we to place intellectual dissent in the

2. Strictly speaking, communism fell in Soviet Russia in January 1991,
when the Russian Supreme Soviet passed the law of "Private Property in the
RSFSR," which permitted capitalism in all branches of the economy, including the hiring of wage earners. See P. G. Pikhoia, *Sovetskii Soiuz: Istoriia
vlasti, 1945–1991* (Moscow, 1998), pp. 573–74. The Soviet Union, however,
survived until the end of the year.

hierarchy of causes? Lenin well understood the need for securing full control of the media; the very first act of the dictatorship that he set up on October 26, 1917, was to assert a monopoly of the Communist Party on the press. His government was as yet too weak to enforce this measure, a throwback to the reign of Nicholas I, but within a few years communist control of the printed word was complete. It was my impression, gained on many trips to the USSR from 1957 onward, that the Soviet authorities did not much care what their subjects thought; their concern was exclusively with what they said. They strove to create a spurious unanimity of opinion in order to convey the sense that dissent from the official line was an aberration, which had the effect of driving independent thought inward, creating a condition akin to intellectual schizophrenia. The regime never came close to enforcing unanimity of opinion, but it was eminently successful in eliminating any public expressions of dissent from the officially sanctioned "line."

Immediately after Stalin's death, when his successors began to loosen the bonds of censorship, information about the country and the world at large began to seep in, first in a trickle, then in a stream, and finally in a torrent. Why they relaxed the censorship is not clear, but it must assumed they thought they could do so with endangering their authority. And for a while this was true. But unexpectedly in the 1960s there emerged independent voices of dissidence that confronted the regime head on. In the 1970s, following the signing of the Helsinki accords, in which the USSR committed itself to tolerating a certain amount of freedom in exchange for foreign guarantees of its European empire, these voices became bolder. Amplified by foreign broadcasts that, despite intense jamming, managed to get through, they broke the spell. With each passing year, fewer Soviet citizens were afraid to speak out. By the late 1980s, censorship broke down altogether and a remarkably diffuse range of opinion burst into the open. Here then we have three more causes of the Soviet Union's collapse, each contributing its share, although it would be a futile exercise to try to determine which carried greater weight.

Last but not least among factors of this nature must be mentioned the policy of containment pursued by the United States jointly with its allies from 1947 until the Soviet regime's end. It was only partly successful. With the conquest of China by the Communists in 1949, the communist empire broke out of its Soviet enclave. Subsequently, pro-Soviet regimes, subsidized and propped by Moscow, sprang up in other parts of Asia, in Africa, and in Latin America. Still, the determination of the Western powers, especially the United States, to thwart this expansion cost Moscow dearly. The large sums spent on financing proxy regimes made a serious dent in the Soviet budget, strained as it already was, while the break with China cast doubts on the claims of communist unity and the unstoppable advance of the communist cause.

On reflection, however, the decisive catalyst—the cause of causes, the one that ensured that the Soviet regime would fall sooner or later, whether slowly and gradually, or suddenly, no matter what it did and no matter what was done to it—appears to have lain deeper still. It was the utopian nature of its objectives.

When in everyday speech we use the adjective *utopian* we mean something that "is too good to be true," in the words of the dictionary, something "impossibly ideal." But, as a matter of fact, virtually all utopias depicted an environment of dreary coercion in which the citizens lived under unrelenting control and faced dire punishment for disobedience. R. W. Chambers has rightly observed that "few books have been more misunderstood than More's *Utopia*":

It has given the English language a word "Utopian" to signify something visionary and unpractical. Yet the remarkable thing about *Utopia* is the extent to which it adumbrates social and political reforms which have either been actually carried into practice, or which have come to be regarded as very practical politics. *Utopia* is depicted as a sternly righteous and puritanical State, where few of us would feel quite happy; yet we go on using the word "Utopia" to signify an easy-going paradise, whose only fault is that it is too happy and ideal to be realized.[3]

Suffice it to say that the denizens of More's ideal community not only lived in identical houses and dressed alike, they not only could not travel without permission, they not only suffered enslavement for adultery, but they were liable to be executed for taking "counsel on matters of common interest" (i.e., discussing politics in private).

Why utopias are coercive presents no mystery. Their common striving is to dissolve individual human beings in the community in order to achieve perfect equality: Plato wanted not only to abolish all property and nationalize, as it were, wives and children but to bring into being a society

in which the private and individual is altogether banished from life, and things which are by nature private, such as eyes and ears and hands, have become common, and in some way see and hear and act in common.[4]

3. *Thomas More* (London, 1935), p. 125. Alexander Gray goes even further, saying that "no utopia has ever been described in which any sane man would on any conditions consent to live": *The Socialist Tradition* (London, 1947), p. 62.
4. "The Laws," in B. Jowett, ed., *The Dialogues of Plato*, V (Oxford, 1892), pp. 121–22.

This may be an extreme formulation, but it is one shared in some way by all designers of utopias.

Experience indicates that it is impossible to attain such a condition except by coercion and even then for a limited time only. The problem with utopian schemes is that they presume to determine what people *should* want rather than respond to what they actually *do* want. And since, beyond basic survival of themselves and their families, people's wants vary enormously, force must be applied to have them want the same. This is why utopian communities have always failed and why such communities imposed from above rather than formed voluntarily are even more liable to failure.

The experiment at utopia launched in Russia in October 1917 was the grandest, most audacious attempt in human history completely to refashion society and individuals, to create a "new man," and in the process to subvert virtually the entire heritage of human history. The question arises: Why was this attempt made and why, of all places, in Russia?

The intellectual roots of socialist utopianism lie embedded in the philosophy of the Enlightenment, specifically in the philosophic notion that human beings are composed entirely of matter and that their ideas and feelings are the product of sensory perceptions. The rejection by the *philosophes* of the traditional view of the duality of body and soul led logically to the notion that human beings can be molded and remolded at will. Claude Helvétius, a follower of John Locke, believed that it was quite possible so to reconstruct humans that they could not help but be "virtuous."

This perception influenced profoundly the social and political thought of modern times. Through Jeremy Bentham it penetrated liberal thought and, through Marx, the ideology of socialism. Liberal thought placed its reliance on legislation and instruction, that is, on nonviolent means of transforming human personalities and behavior. Socialism was prone to rely on violence because it assumed that the decisive factor in history was property relations and that no permanent changes could be effected without the abolition of private property in the means of production. This required coercion since the owners would not willingly give up their belongings. In the West, where the traditions of legality and property were strong, socialism over time tended to lose its revolutionary character and turn into evolutionary Social-Democracy.

It was different in Russia and other non-Western countries where these traditions were missing or weakly developed. Here, socialism acquired at once a coercive character, blending with the legacy of autocratic rule and hostility to property. No European socialist would have defined the "proletarian dictatorship" as did Lenin to mean "nothing else than power that is limited by nothing, by no laws, that is restrained by absolutely no rules, that rests directly on coercion."[5] There were no bounds to the Bolsheviks' ambition because there was no culture of moderation in Russia and no society able to resist effectively their plans to remake the country from top to bottom.

Lenin was aware that the violence that he intended to apply to alter fundamentally human nature had its limits. In a secret communication to the Politburo written in March 1922 in which he ordered mass executions of Orthodox clergymen, he noted:

> One wise writer on matters of statecraft [the reference is to Machiavelli] rightly said that if it is necessary to resort to certain brutalities, they must be carried out in the most en-

5. V. I. Lenin, *Polnoe sobranie sochinenii*, 5th ed. (Moscow, 1958–65), vol. 41, p. 383.

ergetic fashion and in the briefest possible time because the
masses will not tolerate the prolonged application of brutality.[6]

Unfortunately for him and his successors, the application
of "brutality"—in other words, terror—never succeeded in creating the "new man" or the new society that was its avowed
aim. Terror, therefore, became a regular component of the government apparatus, creating a condition of permanent tension
between state and society.

In their pursuit of utopia, the Communists violated everything we know from anthropology that human beings, even in
the most primitive circumstances, desire and practice. They
virtually outlawed religion, property, and free speech, which
are common to all societies, regardless of their level of civilization.[7] Any regime that deliberately sets out to repress these
institutions is inherently unstable and therefore prone to be
fatally affected by adverse developments, whether of an incidental or substantive nature, developments that normal societies readily absorb.

If this is so why then did experts on the Soviet Union—
practitioners of so-called Sovietology—not foresee its fall? I do
not mean the date and circumstances of its sudden demise,
which were determined by the incidental factors alluded to
previously. I rather mean why did they not grasp the inherent
weaknesses of the communist regime, its susceptibility to
shocks, whether generated internally or externally? The pro-
fession was all but unanimous that the Soviet Union, which
had weathered countless challenges in the past, would also

6. Richard Pipes, ed., *The Unknown Lenin* (New Haven, Conn., 1996),
p. 153.
7. See Clark Wissler, *Man and Culture* (New York, 1923), pp. 74–75.

cope with its economic crisis as well as the clamor of the nationalities and the discontent of the intellectuals.

When I served in the White House in 1981–82, Secretary of State Alexander Haig, as well as his successor, George Shultz, equally opposed the aggressive anticommunism of President Reagan and the measures that he activated to speed its demise. To gain authoritative support for their positions, they convened meetings of "experts" to advise them on the effectiveness of the economic sanctions against the Soviet Union that the U.S. government had imposed following the introduction of Martial Law in Poland. Secretary Haig subsequently reported to the National Security Council that his experts assured him "it was 'crazy' to think we could 'bust' the Soviet Union," that country was in trouble but there was no hope of changing its system by means of economic warfare. Shultz received similar advice.

I have given much thought to this professional obtuseness without arriving at a definitive answer. It seems likely that ultimately the reason for the failure of the professionals to understand the Soviet predicament lay in their indifference to the human factor. In the desire to emulate the successes of the natural scientists, whose judgments are "value-free," politology and sociology have been progressively dehumanized, constructing models and relying on statistics (many of them falsified) and, in the process, losing contact with the subject of their inquiries—the messy, contradictory, unpredictable *homo sapiens*. Anyone who spent an hour walking the streets of Moscow, the Soviet Union's richest city, with open eyes, would have dismissed as preposterous CIA statistics showing the Soviet gross domestic product as well as its living standards to be nearly half of the United States. Talking to Soviet citizens with an open mind would have revealed that the appearance of widespread support for the regime was fraudulent.

Such evidence, however, was generally dismissed as "anec-dotal" and hence unworthy of serious attention.

The few people who did predict the fall of communism were almost without exception amateurs, usually of a conser-vative persuasion. They evaluated the situation without pre-tence at "science," applying common sense and allowing for moral factors that the experts studiously avoided. Thus in 1950 James Burnham published *The Coming Defeat of Com-munism*. Michel Garder, a professional officer of the French army, wrote in 1965 about the *Agonie du régime en Russie soviétique*. Andrei Amalrik predicted that the catastrophe would occur by 1984, the year of Orwell's anti-utopian novel. Garder may have gotten his date wrong—he thought the agony would end in death by 1970—and Amalrik gave the wrong reason for it (war with China), but both did anticipate correctly the outcome. In 1976 a brilliant young French demographer, Emmuanel Todd, predicted the inevitable demise of the Soviet Union because personal contact with Soviet citizens—the very "anecdotal" evidence scorned by experts—convinced him it was a very sick society.[8] And what of President Reagan's repeated public assurances that the end of communism was near—assurances dismissed at the time as hallucinations of a "Cold Warrior"?

Is the inquiry into the reasons for the collapse of the Soviet Union and the failure of the experts to foresee it of any signif-icance? It surely is—both retrospectively and prospectively.

It matters for historians because the collapse of the Soviet Union sheds light on the collapse three-quarters of a century earlier of the tsarist regime. Since the 1960s it has become fashionable among Russian historians in the West to depict

---

8. *La chute finale* (Paris: Editions Robert Laffont, 1976); translated as *The Final Fall* (New York: Karz Publishers, 1979).

the end of tsarism as the consequence of mounting pressures from "below." But it is now apparent that a seemingly indestructible Russian government could collapse instantaneously without such pressures. In 1991 there were no riots, no mutinies, no barricades—indeed no mass violence; such demonstrations as took place and expressed public discontent with the status quo were legal assemblies in support of liberal candidates for the new Congress of People's Deputies of the USSR. There were crises of various kinds, to be sure, of both the incidental and the systemic variety, but they certainly could have been kept under control for some time to come were it not for the loss of confidence and direction on the part of the leadership. So it seems a revolution can occur from "above." This is additional reason to give up the old Marxist notion that all history is a history of "class struggles" that politics merely echos.

As concerns the professions of political science and sociology, if they have any claims to being scientific disciplines, as their names imply, they certainly ought to engage in vigorous self-criticism to determine what went wrong. This they have failed so far to do. Such a methodological postmortem is essential lest they commit similar errors in the future. The national intelligence community depends heavily on the academe for analytic methodology and tends to replicate its conclusions. Hence, academics' mistakes can, indirectly, exert a very detrimental influence on the advice given to the decision makers and on the policies they pursue as a result.

4

The
Stalin Era

Robert Conquest

I

THE THIRTY YEARS between Lenin's incapacitation in 1923 and Stalin's death in 1953 saw the effective consolidation, by terror, of the single-party totalitarian system and the command economy, and also the institutionalizing of what George Orwell (basing himself on the Soviet system), called "doublethink"—that is to say, the radical falsification, in every public medium, of the unpleasant realities. Moreover, as the Stalinists achieved complete power in Moscow, they took over, as a consequence, control of the international communist movement, and of its vast, and Soviet-financed, machinery for misinforming the world in general both about the true state of things in the USSR and about the motives and intentions of its leadership.

II

Lenin's illness and death found the party and the country in a state of utter exhaustion. Civil war, peasant war and famine, and all the disastrous policies of the Bolsheviks, had done enormous economic and demographic damage. The party, over the years since the revolution, had been faced with intense opposition not merely from the peasantry, but also from the proletarians whose representative it claimed to be. It had by then long lost any serious basis in any social stratum except its own ranks.

The attempts to bring down the regime had failed. But the peasantry, defeated in its numerous rebellions, had nevertheless shown that for the party to pursue the true Bolshevik program was, for now at least, bound to result in the collapse of the regime. As a result a measure of economic normality, of relaxation, was to a fair degree pacifying the country.

Politically, however, the key fact was that the Bolsheviks having, by the skin of their teeth, kept power, had not changed their long-term aims.

By this time all non-communist political movements in Russia had been crushed, and it was only within the party that any disputes over power and policy could now emerge. The rulers who now found themselves in charge of the party and the country were in effect a few hundred veterans of an extreme millenarian underground sect. The mass membership which they controlled were political cannon fodder with little say. And the future of the state depended on discussion and dispute within a leadership known for ruthlessness rather than rationality.

They were faced with ideological as well as practical problems. For one thing, the Bolsheviks had, contrary to the Marxism they professed, taken power in a backward, non-proletarianized country, claiming that this was only plausible as the forerunner of revolutions in the West. With this in mind they had sponsored an array of communist parties, some small, some large, but all capable of troublesome action in their respective countries.

Lenin's creation, the Comintern, depended from the start on Soviet subventions, together with organizational and other help by its Moscow promoters, which gave it and its component parties a huge advantage over other radical groups or parties—all, moreover, subjected to the Bolshevik organizational principle of "democratic centralism," which in effect meant quasi-military obedience to orders. In addition, they were all permeated by the narrow, sectarian, and life-hostile ideological requirements of membership. Nor should we forget how they contributed to the stultification of their adepts. Richard Wright, for a time a member of the Communist Party of the United States (CPUSA), was to say in his *American Hunger*:

> An hour's listening disclosed the fanatical intolerance of minds sealed against new ideas, new facts, new feelings, new attitudes, new hints at ways to live. They denounced books they had never read, people they had never known, ideas they could never understand, and doctrines they could not pronounce. Communism, instead of making them leap forward with fire in their hearts . . . had frozen them at an even lower level of ignorance than had been theirs before they met Communism.

But by 1924, plans for the immediate revolutionizing of the West had failed. So the Bolsheviks now had, in practice, to abandon either their theory or their power. As ever in such circumstances, power won out. But, for such an ideology-addicted sect, theory too had to be adjusted or finessed.

It was in this context that Stalin advanced the concept of "Socialism in One Country." This was a mental wrench for some Bolsheviks, but provided power with its excuse—advanced, moreover, by a figure who already had a large measure of control over appointments and votes. On this and other issues Stalin consolidated his position over a post-Lenin period when, for a time, the Communists had no recognized leader. A bitter struggle naturally ensued. Over the next five years, Stalin defeated first Trotsky, then the Zinoviev-Kamenev "Left," and finally his allies in those struggles, the Bukharin-Rykov "Right." By the end of 1930, Trotsky had been expelled from the country and all Stalin's remaining opponents had been removed from power and had submitted.

But the Communists, during the middle and late 1920s, were still faced with the question of what to do in Russia itself. Over the period of temporarily muted struggle with the citizenry, Stalin had been building up his political and police control. It was in the late 1920s too that the falsificatory atmosphere was developed, as in the 1928 "Shakhty" trial of engineers charged with sabotage in the service of the class enemy.

Increasing pressure was put on the peasantry, and then—against Bukharin, Rykov, and others—Stalin felt strong enough to launch what he called a "revolution from above," a new offensive to create the "socialism" which had had to be abandoned in 1921.

A "planned economy" was promulgated; and the decision was taken to bring the peasantry under complete economic and political control. In the interim, it should be noted the party had practiced what was only a comparative restraint compared with the ferocity of earlier and later periods. The campaign against religion continued. The Marxist class war dogmas continued too. "Bourgeois" specialists in the economy, the academy, and elsewhere, who had been necessary while communist substitutes were being trained, were removed in a "cultural revolution." (The new engineers were not, in fact, adequately trained, and much damage resulted.) All this was intensified, and from 1929 on we see the full development of the Soviet system we associate with Stalin.

III

The collectivization and dekulakization now inflicted on the country are seen in two aspects. The independent peasantry were reduced to a "new serfdom," as they often put it, of complete subordination to the communist state, herded, with their farms and livestock, into collectives under party-appointed bosses.

At the same time, as was to be the case in similar circumstances in other communist countries, the whole operation was represented as voluntary and part of a class struggle against a supposedly richer stratum, the so-called kulak.

This term of opprobrium was applied in the nineteenth century to rural moneylenders, usually one to a group of villages. In 1918 Lenin applied it to a small stratum having some eighty acres, who were then liquidated. Stalin applied it to peasants with a horse and a couple of cows; in practice it was used of any peasant offering serious resistance to the party's emissaries. Above all, it was a Marxist, or pseudo-Marxist, class justification for terror in the countryside. From early 1930, after mass shootings, millions of kulaks were deported in inhuman circumstances to the Arctic, where survivors lived miserably in secret police settlements.

Meanwhile, in the villages, mass collectivization of those remaining was enforced. The first effort was admittedly a debacle. A major result had been the slaughter by the peasants of half of the country's livestock—a disaster on an unprecedented scale. And in March 1930 Stalin ordered a retreat. Of the fourteen million families that had been "voluntarily" collectivized, the great majority now left.

Over the next two years, by a more carefully prepared combination of physical and economic pressure, the peasants were again collectivized. The crop much diminished (though from now on falsified figures on it were published). And the state exacted whatever grain it regarded as its entitlement. At the end of 1932 and in 1933, a famine ensued, especially in Ukraine. It resulted purely and simply from the communist overseers seizing all the available grain. The party secretary of the key Dnepropetrovsk Province, Mikhail Khataevich, wrote to Molotov in November 1932 that if agriculture was to flourish "we need to take into account the minimum needs of the collective farmers, otherwise there will be no one left to sow and to ensure production." Molotov answered, "Your position is profoundly incorrect, not Bolshevik. We Bolsheviks cannot put the needs of the State . . . in the tenth, or even the second place."

Apart from state resources, more than enough grain had been exported to have prevented starvation. As it was some 6–7 million people died—a figure comparable to the 8–9 million dead *in all countries* in World War I. As to the official story, not only did Moscow deny abroad that any famine had occurred, but in the USSR itself, even in the worst-hit areas, to mention the word *famine* was treated as anti-Soviet propaganda and a cause for instant arrest.

IV

With the population thoroughly crushed, and the country brought socially, politically, and economically under the control of the communist state, it began to look as if some sort of authoritarian normality might be possible. Even among the ranks of the Stalinist Central Committee there was such a mood. The Stalinists, victorious over the people and the oppositionists alike, had in many cases themselves become exhausted by the intensity of the struggle. Among the delegates of the Seventeenth Congress of the Communist Party of the Soviet Union (CPSU) in February 1934—the "Congress of Victors"—these attitudes emerged in suggestions, reported to Stalin by informers, that his ruthlessness, however necessary it had been, was now inappropriate. He was told this directly by Politburo member Sergei Kirov, one of his firmest supporters, who had lately been among those opposing harsh measures against "oppositionists" in the party.

On December 1, 1934, Kirov was killed in circumstances that point strongly to Stalin's agents having enabled the assassin to carry out his plan. The following day a decree was issued providing for the trial and immediate execution of "terrorists," and on December 3 more than a hundred of these were shot. Heavily printed headlines announced their fate in the Soviet newspapers (since rehabilitated, they seem to have been a random selection of people in jail for lesser offenses).

The actual assassin was interrogated and, with a number of ex-oppositionists named as his accomplices, was shot after a closed trial at the end of December. And Stalin's old opponents in the party, Zinoviev and Kamenev, were jailed for indirect responsibility for the crime. Over the next year a vast "plot" was discovered in the Kremlin itself, and scores of librarians, cleaning people, and other suspects were jailed or shot.

V

Meanwhile, the Stalinists had been active on the international scene. By the end of the 1920s they had removed their opponents not only from the Soviet leadership but also from the Comintern. Henceforward that organization was simply a servile tool of Stalin and the Moscow Politburo.

In the late 1920s and early 1930s its line was that the worst enemy of the Communists were the socialist and social democratic parties in the West, always spoken of as "Social-fascists." And though nazi and communist street fighters had clashed fiercely in Germany, the German Communist Party acted jointly with the Nazis in the referendum of 1931 and the transport strike of 1932. When Hitler, in part as the result of communist sabotage of the antifascist ranks, came to power, the communist line was that capitalism had been driven into fascism as a desperate last stand and would soon be overthrown. Instead, the German Communists were suppressed without difficulty, and many of them went over to the Nazis.

In 1934, the Comintern line changed again, and from then until 1939 the central drive was for "People's Fronts" in the capitalist countries. These coalitions of Communists, Socialists, and Liberals formed governments in France and Spain in 1936. In Spain, the Civil War ensued, and many in other Western countries became strong supporters of Republican resistance to Franco, with the Communists getting a large share of the credit. Stalin supported them to the extent of military equipment and the rallying of some tens of thousands of sympathizers, mainly communist, into the International Brigades on the Republican side.

The Spanish Communists were greatly encouraged and strengthened, and the non-communist left, associated in Stalin's view with Trotskyism, was repressed by force, as described by George Orwell in his *Homage to Catalonia*. NKVD agents operated freely against non-Stalinist International Brigaders. The Spanish communist leaders, some reluctantly, were put under direct orders from Soviet agents and in general forced the Stalinist policies on their government. It has lately been shown that, while the Spanish gold reserves were shipped to the USSR never to return, the actual supply of Soviet arms was comparatively meager. And by mid-1938, evidently seeing that Republican victory was a mirage, Moscow lost interest.

Stalin's motives have often been questioned. The most plausible, given the immense emphasis placed on the communist struggle against Trotskyites on the one hand and respectable left-wing politicians unamenable to Soviet control on the other, seems to be that Stalin wanted above all to prevent the establishment of an antifascist regime independent of Moscow.

The collapse of the Spanish Republic in 1939 was followed later that year by the Nazi-Soviet Pact. Secretly negotiated and announced without warning, it was a test of Stalin's control of communist parties everywhere. With few exceptions, they passed that test. In all the Western countries they organized opposition to the Allied war effort and called for a "People's Peace." The leading theorist of the British CP, Palme Dutt, was writing a book to that theme in June 1941. But the line changed again with Hitler's attack on Russia, and it had to be rewritten in favor of out-and-out war.

The Comintern was officially dissolved in 1943, but the non-Soviet communist parties continued to be controlled and heavily funded from Moscow, in some cases (in the United States and France) well into the 1980s.

VI

Early in 1936, the NKVD began to fabricate a vast underground Trotskyite plot, and soon the former "leftist" leaders were brought from their jails to Moscow and integrated into this fictitious conspiracy. By July, by a variety of physical and other pressures, confessions had been obtained from most of the accused, including these former communist paragons, who agreed to go to trial after guarantees that if they publicly confessed they would not be shot but if they refused they would be tried in secret and executed. After a trial conducted with vast publicity, they were all shot.

This was the first of the famous "Moscow Trials" of ex-oppositionists charged with killing Kirov and plotting to kill Stalin and others. Not only was it a public spectacle, but thereafter the theme of huge enemy conspiracies was hammered in daily and hourly by the entire Soviet media. The pressures were kept up. Hundreds of ex-oppositionists were shot in secret, and in January 1937 came the second public Moscow Trial, at which Pyatakov and others confessed not merely to terrorism, but also to treason, espionage, and sabotage. A few days later Stalin's oldest and closest colleague, Sergo Ordzhonikidze, committed suicide (or was murdered), and the following week the decisive "February–March Plenum" of the Central Committee endorsed terror, and saw the arrest of Bukharin, Rykov, and former "Rightist" leaders.

At this point Stalin had established that any shred of opposition or mere allegation of opposition to his rule would result in arrest, torture, and execution. The atmosphere in the whole country became, even more than before, one of fear and hysteria. And even Stalinist officials with no record of resistance to him now disappeared.

In late May 1937, eight leading generals were arrested, to

be shot as Nazi agents in June. The purge of the armed forces that followed led to the execution of almost the entire leading cadre of the Soviet army and navy and a disastrous decrease in military efficiency; it takes years of experience to produce a good army or corps commander. What was the rationale for what appears, on the face of it, to be an act of insanity? Stalin seems to have regarded the military as a potentially alternative source of power. And we can add that, evidently, once leading officers were arrested, their colleagues at liberty would almost automatically be taken in as accomplices, under the general logic of the unrestrained police terror.

In June a plenum of the Central Committee giving even greater power to the NKVD saw a last attempt by a few members to restrain Stalin. They were arrested; and over the next year or so most of the committee members were shot in closed "trials."

This was accompanied by decrees launching a massive terror against the population as a whole. The main victims up to mid-1937 had been from the party itself and the army. The new decrees sent quotas for mass arrest and execution to all the provinces. The figures were, moreover, continually increased, and after they were implemented a new and even larger quota was ordered early in 1938. Everywhere anyone who could possibly be charged as alien to the regime filled the local jails and graveyards.

Concentration camps had existed since the early years of the regime. In the 1930s they became institutionalized on a vast scale in the Chief Administration of Camps (Gulag), which evolved into a network of nearly five hundred camp groups over the whole country, though especially and most lethally in the far north. Here, over the whole period, millions slaved on inadequate rations, with a high death toll.

To sum up this whole period, and its long-term effects: not

only was there a huge demographic catastrophe, with millions
of excess deaths, but many who survived lost years of their
lives in labor camps. And the whole population was put into a
long lasting state of extreme repression. As the Soviet writer
Vasily Grossman told of it,

> This fear that millions of people find insurmountable,
> this fear written up in crimson letters over the leaden
> sky of Moscow—this terrible fear of the state . . .

Moreover, those who replaced the victims in the state, the
economic, and also the cultural sphere represented a degrada-
tion of the whole of society. The physicist Alexander Weiss-
berg noted in the economic sphere:

> They were the men who had denounced others on innumer-
> able occasions. They had bowed the knee whenever they had
> come up against higher authority. They were morally and
> intellectually crippled.

As a Soviet periodical complained in 1988, all this was "the
conscious result of negative selection, of the horrible social
selection which went on in this country for decades." And
while the ruling apparatus thus became more and more stulti-
fied and vicious, the representatives of culture, truth, and humanity were silenced and repressed. Hundreds of writers, po-
ets, dramatists, historians, and philosophers ended their lives
in the camps or the execution cellars.

VII

The other considerable success of the Stalinists was, as we
have said, the projection on much of the Western and Third

World intelligentsia not only of Marxist-Leninist views of their own country but also of a wholly or largely false view of the mere facts of the Soviet experience.

When it came to the picture represented abroad, where the USSR had thousands of propaganda agents and far more dupes, this fake was perpetrated on a huge scale—and even up to the 1990s there were people in the West (mostly academics) who did not accept that Trotsky's assassin was an NKVD agent, or that the Russians were guilty of the Katyn massacre. Even today there are powerful, or at any rate loud, voices, telling us that even if Stalin was ruthless, he "modernized" Russia, a patent falsehood: and even when confined to the supposed success of crash industrialization, those voices rely on old Stalinist statistics, long dismissed by Russia and Western researchers alike.

VIII

For several years Stalin had kept up confidential contact with nazi circles. As he had said publicly at the Seventeenth Party Congress in 1934, he hoped for better relations with Germans.

By this time official Soviet policy was one of alliance with France and "collective security." Much Soviet diplomatic effort was put into this, though, as Robert C. Tucker puts it, Stalin "worked for the formation of a strong politico-military anti-German grouping based on France and Britain. But, it was not a coalition in which he wanted the Soviet Union to participate when war came."

The other option of agreement with Germany was kept open, and around the end of May 1939, the Germans decided to take Moscow up on this. France and Britain had nothing to offer but alliance in a dangerous war, while Hitler was able to propose peace and a large accession of territory to the Soviet Union. In August the Soviet-German pact was signed. Hitler invaded Poland a week later, and Stalin attacked that country on September 17, by which time military resistance had all but ceased.

In the USSR the pact had various results. Much economic cooperation with the Nazis ensued. The use of the term *fascist* in a hostile sense in the Soviet media was banned on Stalin's direct order. A U-boat base for operations against Britain was set up near Murmansk—which never became operational only because the British sank the two U-boats heading for it—and it became superfluous from the nazi point of view after their invasion of Norway. The Soviets were able to help, however, by escorting the German warship *Komet* through the Arctic Sea route to the Pacific, where it did much damage to Allied shipping.

The pact had made the Baltic States part of the Soviet sphere. In November 1939 heavy Soviet pressure forced these countries to accept Soviet military and naval bases; in June 1940 they were annexed to the USSR after a pseudo-election. Deportation and executions followed on a large scale.

Meanwhile an ultimatum to Finland had been rejected, and the period from December 1939 to March 1940 saw the "Winter War." After a series of Finnish victories, massive Red Army assaults broke through, but Soviet fear of Allied intervention led to the scrapping of a puppet communist government and a compromise peace.

It was in March, too, that one of the most indefensible of all Stalin's crimes took place, one which was to have international repercussions for fifty years. He ordered the execution of fifteen thousand Polish prisoners of war and some thousands of civilian Poles in what has become known as the Katyn massacre, after one of the secret mass graves into which they were piled. Discovered and publicized by the Germans in 1943, Soviet propaganda—right up until 1990—attributed the murders to the Nazis.

A few months later came a murder of a different type. Pacts with such as Hitler were acceptable to Stalin, but there was one enemy—Trotsky—with whom any accommodation was ruled out, and he was now killed by an NKVD assassin at his home in Mexico. The Trotskyite movement that had emerged in the West was small and weak, with little direct influence. Its constant and public exposure of the Stalinist falsehoods, however, had been a major hindrance to the Soviet projection of falsehood the world over.

Over 1940 to 1941, Stalin continued to observe the pact, and a meeting between Hitler and Molotov in Berlin in November 1940 provisionally divided the spoils expected after the defeat of Britain—the USSR claiming territories southward to the Persian Gulf.

The Nazis were now, however, preparing their attack on Russia. By early June 1941 it was obvious to both Western and Soviet intelligence that this was imminent. Stalin, however, refused to credit it. He seems to have decided that it could not happen for at least a year.

The nazi attack thus found the USSR ill prepared, and they inflicted a series of defeats on a Soviet army deprived of trained leadership by the purges and reached the outskirts of Leningrad and Moscow. Stalin intervened, often disastrously, in military decisions but finally allowed his generals to decide on strategy with good results (just when Hitler was in turn imposing inept orders on his own generals). Stalin never ceased, however, to insist on tactics involving large and unnecessary Soviet losses.

World War II was a profound and tragic experience for the Soviet people, who suffered more than twenty million dead.

At the same time, it is often described as to some degree "liberating" in the sense that they were no longer passive victims but were fighting back. As Stalin himself said, the Russians were "fighting for their homeland, not for us."

For the war's duration, Stalin fell back on appeals to the deeper Russian patriotism, and to collaboration with the Orthodox Church—all in all, a sort of ideological N.E.P. And, once again, the communist shift of tactics did not involve any relaxation of their grip in power. As it was, the millions of Soviet prisoners of war captured by the Nazis were disavowed. If they were officers their wives were arrested; if rank and file, their wives were merely deprived of their ration books.

And, even with the open anti-Slavic attitudes of the Nazis, a number of high Soviet officers, including several generals, formed a fair-sized anticommunist army on the German side—as happened in no other country attacked by Hitler. Meanwhile, nearly a million prisoners in the Gulag were transferred to penal battalions, which were mainly used for frontal attacks across minefields (over the same time just under a million others died in the Gulag itself).

As the war went on, the Stalinists once again acted on a large scale against supposed internal enemies. More than two million members of suspect nationalities were deported en bloc to Siberia and elsewhere and their republics abolished.

But, in general, Moscow's appeal to patriotism was successful, though even with the splendid resilience of the Russian soldiery, Stalin could hardly have won his war without the supplies sent to the USSR by the West.

Victory brought other problems.

IX

At the end of the war the Soviet Union was exhausted. It was widely expected by its citizens that their efforts and sacrifices would lead to better things. It was felt, too, that the alliance with the West would mean more toleration of Western ideas. But Stalin and the ruling group saw any opening to Western, or non-communist, attitudes as a threat to their position. From early 1946 came a severe cultural purge. Everything Western or liberal or indeed non-communist became suspect. Stalin's spokesman Andrei Zhdanov denounced all pro-Western trends among the intelligentsia. In 1948, after Zhdanov's death, his followers were arrested (and later executed). But the anti-Western trend continued, with the installation of Trofim Lysenko and his absurd theories, as the official bearer of Soviet biological science—the period's worst, but by no means its only, blow to the Soviet mind.Some of Stalin's senior advisers had, in 1945, recommended, without in any way abandoning the long-term aims of world communism, that the USSR seek a temporary easing of relations with the West for the next decade or two. After all, Moscow had avoided expansionism from the early 1920s to 1939. But Stalin chose the more aggressive of the available policies—in part, because a tense and overtly xenophobic atmosphere was needed at home, and in Soviet-occupied Eastern Europe.

As the Soviet armies entered that area, they were everywhere used to support local Communists. In Poland, they failed to help the Warsaw Rising organized by the legitimate Polish government's underground representatives. Then in 1945 a Soviet safe conduct was given to the Polish underground leaders, who came to confer but were arrested and jailed. A narrow communist clique was then imposed in Warsaw.

Over the following years, the communist parties all over Eastern Europe were established in power by force and fraud and, once established, followed the Stalinist pattern of intra-party purges, public trials, and mass terror of which we need only note that all the communist phenomena first presented to the world in the USSR were to be seen everywhere in their full negativity. The seizure of power in Czechoslovakia, the Berlin Blockade, and the Korean War faced the West with the prospect of a world under Stalinist attack.

In this unprovoked contest Stalin had certain advantages. His army remained the largest in the world. And he had on his side, or vacillating, a large section of Western society. The two mass communist parties of France and Italy were especially powerful agencies; but everywhere in the West Stalinist views, and misrepresentations, circulated freely, while in the USSR itself Western opinion was totally absent from the media, where the United States and Britain were constantly portrayed as bloodthirsty villains.

On the other hand, first the American monopoly of the nuclear weapon, and later American superiority in bombers, meant that direct attack was ruled out. And (as Stalin saw) the American economy was vastly more powerful. As to the effect of Stalin's massive propaganda, with huge subventions to so-called peace movements, a few Western writers, such as Orwell and Koestler, were to a great extent fighting the efforts of Moscow to a standstill.

x

The postwar period in the Soviet Union itself was marked above all by an ideological xenophobia, which included an increasingly vicious, and increasingly overt, anti-Semitism. First, Jewish figures in the arts were criticized and removed.

The USSR's leading Jewish figure, the actor-producer Solomon Mikhoels, was murdered in 1948 at a secret police dacha by a team headed by the deputy minister, on direct orders from Stalin—though it was reported as a car accident. Mikhoels was given a public funeral. But soon the Jewish Anti-Fascist Committee, which had worked with Jews all over the world during the war, and which he had headed, was dissolved. Its members were tried in secret, after severe torture, and shot in May–August 1952.

Later that year a number of leading Soviet doctors, mostly but not all Jewish, were arrested—and this time their alleged plot to murder the Soviet leaders on behalf of American, British, and Israeli intelligence was given huge publicity. Jews and the Jewish community throughout the country were savagely and continually abused in all the media.

After Stalin's death the doctors were publicly rehabilitated and released, though the Jewish Anti-Fascist Committee members had to wait some years before their names were cleared.

An article in the Moscow journal *Novoe Vremya* (no 14 [April 12, 1998]), by Lev Bezymenski, describes a diary kept by the long-serving Soviet people's commissar and minister Vyacheslav Malyshev in which he notes his meetings with Stalin—in particular a session of the Presidium of the Central Committee, of which he was a member, on December 1, 1952. He quotes Stalin verbatim, as follows, "Every Jew [or "any Jew"—the word is *lyuboy*] is a nationalist, that is an agent of American intelligence. Jew-nationalists consider that their nation was saved by the USA (there it's possible to become rich, bourgeois, etc). They consider themselves obligated to the Americans. Among the doctors are many Jew-nationalists." (This was at the time of the Doctors' Plot.)

XI

When in the midst of this campaign Stalin died in March 1953, he left a country which had been cut off from the West, and from any ideas or values but a narrow dogmatism for a generation.

The huge physical destruction of the best section of the population was, in fact, accompanied by a perhaps even graver disruption of the country's life—the almost successful repression of all decent thought and feeling.

Joseph Berger, former secretary of the Palestine Communist Party, summed up:

> After Stalin, Russia is like a country devastated by nuclear warfare. The destruction is not only physical but also moral and intellectual. To prove this one has only to read the leading Soviet philosophical and economic journals. In these the lack of originality, the low level of thought and the incapacity to understand the problems treated is agonisingly apparent.

It was sometimes said that the German consciousness took centuries to recover from the Thirty Years' War. It is with some such massive and profound catastrophe that the Stalin period should be compared. As Alexander Solzhenitsyn described the problem nearly twenty years ago, it is a matter of coming out "from under the rubble." The way back to civilization is slow and difficult; and so far progress has not been rapid.

5

The Highest Stage
of Socialism

Martin Malia

OF ALL THE REASONS for the collapse of communism, the most basic is that it was an intrinsically nonviable, indeed impossible, project from the beginning. However important in its genesis were the heritage of Russian backwardedness and authoritarianism, or the personal ruthlessness of Lenin and Stalin, it is Marxism that was the decisive factor, the sine qua non, making communism the historically unique phenomenon it was. And the perverse genius of Marxism is to present an unattainable utopia as an infallibly scientific enterprise.

To understand the Soviet collapse, therefore, it is necessary to go back beyond Red October to the emergence of generic socialism in the aftermath of the French Revolution. For socialism came into the world in the 1830s as the expectation of a Second Coming of 1789–1793, a new and final revolution to achieve full human equality and social rationality. Given such aspirations, when this fantasy at last came to power in

1917 it inevitably took itself as the millenial culmination of history, the revolution to end all revolutions. It is only with the fall of the Berlin Wall in 1989, and the collapse of the Soviet system itself in 1991, that it became clear that the communist specter had all along been an insubstantial mirage, and that the revolution to end all revolutions had in fact been modern history's most colossal fraud.

Thus, 1989–1991 is indeed a cardinal turning point in modern history. Without going so far as to call it the end of history *tout court*, it brought the repeal of 1917 and all its works; and, since 1917 was supposed to have marked the repeal of 1789 (through the alleged fulfillment of 1793), 1989–1991 closed the era of modern revolutionary expectations overall. For the first time since that "dawn" in which Wordsworth famously found it "bliss to be alive," humanity has no revolutionary prospects. Indeed, for the first time in two centuries the world is without any ongoing utopia. For not only has communism been dramatically cast on Trotsky's ashheap of history; socialism and social democracy have unobtrusively landed there too, without anyone taking note. The future now offers us an apparent eternity of free markets and constitutional democracy—which is roughly where matters stood after the great breakthrough to modernity of 1789.

To understand socialism's relationship to that modernity, it is first necessary to dispel some perennial misconceptions. Socialism did not emerge primarily as a reaction against the industrial revolution, or more generally "capitalism" (a totalizing term created by socialists only late in the nineteenth century). The specific response to the dislocations of industrialism, rather, was the labor movement, as expressed in trade unions, cooperatives, and other efforts to achieve security in *existing* society. Socialism, on the other hand, is a political movement designed to produce a new society *after* "capitalism." To be sure, in practice the two movements have often overlapped; but just as often they have been in conflict, for they are in fact distinct.

The growth of the socialist political movement, moreover, does not correlate with that of industrialism. On the contrary, socialism's strength has always stood in reverse proportion to that of capitalism, surprising though this may seem. Thus, there never was a socialist movement in what by 1914 was the world's premier industrial society, the United States—a "lack" creating the false problem of "American exceptionalism" that long bedeviled sociologists. And in Europe by 1914 socialism was weakest in the oldest industrial nations, which were also the most precociously democratic, England and France, but it gained in strength under the semiautocratic and aristocratic empires of Central and Eastern Europe, Germany, Austria, and Russia. In short, socialism has prospered in correlation not with "capitalism" but with the survival into the modern era of Old Regime political and social structures. As Tocqueville defined America's real exceptionalism, it "is reaping the results of the democratic revolution taking place among us [Europeans] without experiencing the revolution itself."

A related misconception about socialism is that it represents the class-consciousness of industrial workers. Although there have been notable working-class socialist leaders, such as P. J. Proudhon and August Bebel, the overwhelming majority of the movement's politicians and theorists, beginning with Marx and Engels themselves, have been from "the bourgeois intelligentsia" as both Karl Kautsky and Lenin insisted. The class-consciousness of workers, on the other hand, has usually been what Lenin derisively called trade union "economism," in other words, the labor movement.

THE SOCIALIST SYNDROME

The first component in the syndrome leading to socialism is the idea of "revolution" itself. In the modern sense of a fundamental break with the past and a radical new departure, this idea emerged only between the American and the French Revolutions. Before then, historical change was disguised as a recovery of roots. Thus, in England the Glorious Revolution of 1688 meant a return to the "ancient constitution" of the realm, and the momentous midcentury transformations preceding this "restoration" were articulated in ostensibly timeless religious terms. Even so, this ahistorical perspective bequeathed an important residue to the dynamic modern concept of revolution.

Nineteenth-century radicals (unlike twentieth-century social historians) were acutely conscious of this religious heritage. The socialist Louis Blanc, for example, began his *History of the French Revolution* with the fifteenth-century Hussites and the communist millennialism of their radical Taborite wing. Friedrich Engels saw the Peasant War of 1525 as the prefiguration of the German Revolution of 1848 and the heterodox priest Thomas Müntzer as the "communist" and the "atheist" predecessor of Marx. Kautsky began his history of socialism (after a bow to Plato's *Republic*) with the twelfth-century heretic Arnold of Brescia.

In fact religion was integral to all social change down to 1798. As late as the seventeenth century Cromwell viewed his Commonwealth of the Saints as the prelude to the Second Coming and the consummation of the world—the end of history, premodern style. This millenarian heritage persisted into the American Revolution, which drew ideologically on the "Commonwealth Men" of eighteenth-century British radicalism. Even in the more thoroughly secular French Revolution, behind Voltaire and Rousseau there lurked a millenarian strain deriving from the eighteenth-century Jansenists' opposition to royal absolutism, and as expressed in the revolutionary calendar of 1793 counting mankind's political redemption from year one of the republic. Indeed, a secularized millenarianism—the belief in revolution as the founding of a *novus ordo saeclorum* inherited from 1776–1789—is a second component of the socialist idea.

It is the Americans who first gave the concept of a new order of the ages an unequivocally secular meaning. Yet, since they were lucky enough to consolidate their revolution almost immediately in a stable constitutional order, 1776 produced no cult of revolution as such. This first emerged from events in France, whose vertiginous upheaval had unfolded like an implacable force of nature. Therefore, revolutions henceforth appeared as the way history happens, its "locomotives" in Marx's famous metaphor; and so radicals hoped for and conservatives feared a Second Coming of 1789.

The first such anticipated revolution was in 1830, and its accomplishment was to define the new 1789 as socialist. It did so by a critique of the Great Revolution (and its feeble reflection in 1830), which was now perceived by the left as having fallen woefully short of its proclaimed ideals of liberty, equality, and fraternity. To be sure, 1789 had abolished the legal class hierarchy of the Old Regime's hereditary estates and made the "nation" sovereign in place of the monarch. The Declaration of the Rights of Man and the Citizen had for the first time established the modern principle of the equality of all men before the law, which the Jacobin Republic in 1793 expanded into universal suffrage. In practice, however, these changes brought real liberty only to the minority of citizens who owned property—the bourgeoisie—and social inequality was as omnipresent as before. Indeed, the propertyless mass of the "people" now found their oppression all the more invidious for the grant of formal legal equality. What is more, the liberty proclaimed by 1789 brought the triumph of economic laissez-faire and the destruction of the guild system (together with the social security it had provided), developments paralleled in England through the efforts of Adam Smith and the Benthamites.

In answer to this "bourgeois liberalism," the left after 1830 demanded some measure of redistribution of private property, and its most radical elements sought to abolish it altogether. (In fact, this last option had appeared in 1796, in the wake of the Jacobins' defeat, with the Conspiracy of the Equals of Gracchus Babeuf, an example rediscovered after 1830.) This extreme form of socialism, professed above all by Auguste Blanqui, was called communism. There were of course other, milder forms of socialism, which Marx later termed *utopian*, that did not aim at radical leveling through revolution. These softer forms of socialism believed in "harmony" rather than class struggle, and their programs ranged from voluntary cooperatives to state action for social security.

But whether hard or soft the new ethos of socialism set the agenda for the politics of modernity that has prevailed to the present day. As Tocqueville observed in 1839:

> The gradual development of the equality of conditions is thus a providential fact, it has the principal characteristic of such a phenomenon: it is universal, it is enduring, and it constantly eludes the power of the human will. All events, just as all men, serve to promote its development. Would it be sensible to believe that a social movement whose impetus comes from such depths can be suspended by the efforts of one generation? Can one really think that, after having destroyed aristocracy and the kings, democracy will stop short before the bourgeoisie and the rich.

Tocqueville called this relentless historical drive toward equality "democracy." If one is ruthlessly logical about this supreme value of modernity, one inevitably arrives at the idea of socialism. It is for this reason that socialism, and its highest stage, communism, has exercised such a haunting spell during the past two centuries.

MARX'S INSPIRATION

The pressure of the new socialism produced a veritable revolutionary movement in Atlantic Europe during the years 1830–1848, which was indeed the seedtime of all modern socialist theories. In economically advanced England the electoral reform of 1832 inspired working-class Chartism to press for immediate universal suffrage—in effect, a demand for revolution by legal means. In France, though industry was less advanced, the power of the revolutionary tradition created insurrectionary conditions in Paris and Lyon during 1830–1834 and an attempted coup by Blanqui in 1839. Thereafter, a succession of secret societies kept the insurrectionary tradition alive, thus fueling the buildup to the century's grandest anticipated revolution, 1848.

In the midst of this tension, in 1843 the twenty-five-year-old Karl Marx arrived in Paris as an émigré; in the next two years, with Engels's aid, he developed all the basic coordinates of his system. First expressed in *The German Ideology* of 1845, this system was given a sloganlike condensation in the *Manifesto* of 1848. In other words, the point of departure of Marx's theorizing was not the empirical observation of the mature "bourgeois mode of production," as the monumental proportions of *Capital*, published in 1867, has led most commentators to assume. Marx's inspiration, rather, was a burning desire to bring the looming Anglo-French revolution to laggard Ger-

many, which still lived in the "Middle Ages" under a monar-
chic and aristocratic regime as yet untouched by the "partial
emancipation" achieved by France and England in 1830–1832.

Yet since the standard of modernity had now been raised
from political democracy to socialism, Marx opined that Germany need not repeat 1789; it could telescope the bourgeois
and socialist revolutions into what he would call, in 1850, a
single "permanent revolution." In this view, such a revolution
was possible, first, because France was about to launch the
socialist locomotive and Germany could hitch onto it as it ran;
second, the very poverty of the German present conferred the
advantage of a superior philosophical understanding of history. Germany thus constituted the "theoretical consciousness" of what more advanced nations had already "done." Its
intellectual socialists therefore could consciously orient their
imminent revolution toward the highest objectives of history.

The proletariat, however, would furnish the revolution's
muscle. As Marx declared in 1843 on "discovering" that class:
"the *head* of this [revolutionary] emancipation is *philosophy*,
and its *heart* is the *proletariat*." In other words, for Marx, the
proletariat was in the first instance a metaphysical category,
not flesh-and-blood workers. As the most exploited and hence
the most dehumanized class of existing society, it became the
class to end all classes because its emancipation would automatically destroy all class inequality. It was thus "the universal class because its sufferings were universal," the only class
whose particular interest coincides with the interests of humanity as a whole. This was hardly abstract humanitarianism,
however, since the obverse of the proletariat's sanctification
was a veritable hatred of backward peasants and the "idiocy of
rural life."

It has often been noted that historically Marxism has tri-
umphed not in advanced countries, as Marx himself expected,

but in backward ones. This outcome is usually explained by the fact that Marxism's cult of progress through industrialization unexpectedly served as an instrument for the crash modernization of rural nations. But this is no accident; Marxism was born as the expectation of a great leap forward out of German backwardness. Marx's "permanent revolution" thus anticipates Lenin's and Trotsky's telescoped 1917 and even its ultimate caricature, Mao Zedong's Great Leap Forward.

Similarly, Marx adumbrated Lenin's avant-garde party of intellectuals in charging the proletariat with the mission of realizing the promises of philosophy. For this philosophy was Hegel's secularization of Christian Providence as the logic of history. In this view, history was a conflictual but rational progression to the absolute self-consciousness of divine reason, a self-consciousness that was also the plentitude of human freedom. For this goal Marx substituted the egalitarian freedom of communism, which was also the plentitude of reason in history. With this overarching metaphysics Marx molded the raw material of British political economy and French revolutionary socialism into a universal system that no Anglo-French radicalism could match.

Concretely, Marx's appropriation of Hegel gave his own system two main axes. First, there was the logic of history leading implacably from slaveholding society to feudalism, to capitalism, to socialism. This "lawlike" rationality of history was in effect the Enlightenment idea of progress expressed in socioeconomic terms. Second, there was the revolutionary consciousness this process was supposed to generate in the proletariat, a consciousness that would ignite the socialist revolution; the anticipated contents of this consciousness were, of course, the tenets of Marx's system. But what would happen if the logic of history did not generate the appropriate consciousness? The answer to this question would not emerge until the century's close.

THE DICTATORSHIP OF THE PROLETARIAT

Eighteen forty-eight ended the active revolutionary movement in Western Europe. The last flare-up of Parisian insurrection, the Commune of 1871, was basically a fluke, due to the Franco-Prussian War. Marx attempted to revive the hopes of 1848 with the First International of 1864–1873, but this was a failure. Even so, by his death in 1883 his system had won out over Proudhon's in France, Ferdinand Lasalle's in Germany, and Michael Bakunin's in Southern Europe. By the 1890s socialism almost everywhere meant Marxism, and even where Marxism was not the official party ideology, as in England, it was regarded as the preeminent socialist theory. This was because of a lifetime of organizational activity by Marx and Engels, to the monumental corpus of their scholarship, and, finally, to the European ascendancy after 1870 of the German Reich, which served to project the strength of its socialist movement and labor unions.

What did Marxism triumphant stand for in practical terms? The literature on this subject is more often than not misleading, since it is predominantly directed toward sanitizing Second International Marxism and excluding bolshevism from the movement's true canon. Thus, it is often said that Marx, unlike utopian socialists, offered no blueprint for the future communist society but only the general laws of history leading to it. In particular, he used the expression "dictatorship of the proletariat" only rarely. Moreover, in 1872 he declared that a parliamentary path to communism might exist; Engels in the last year of his life, 1895, repeated this opinion. What is not mentioned in such arguments is that parliament was supposed to implement the maximalist vision of the *Manifesto*.

This vision consisted in a violent revolution in the manner of 1789 or 1848, and both Marx and Engels to the end of their days were convinced that revolution was imminent. In seizing state power, resorting to proletarian dictatorship was inevitable since "violence is the midwife of history." The program this dictatorship would implement is spelled out unambiguously in part 2 of the *Manifesto*: "Proletarians and Communists." Therein the proletariat is summoned to use its dictatorship to "wrest, by degrees, all capital from the bourgeoisie" and then to "centralize all instruments of production in the hands of the State, i.e., of the proletariat organized as the ruling class." All production, moreover, would be "concentrated in the hands of the vast association of the whole nation" with "industrial armies, especially for agriculture," and a common plan for clearing new land. In short, "the theory of Communism may be summed up in a single sentence: Abolition of private property." Anyone who sees in this program the rough draft of Stalin's first Five-Year Plan would not be mistaken.

In sum, Marx's communism entailed the absolute "negation" of private property, profit, and the market—indeed of money itself. All these opinions, as well as Marx's vehement hostility to the "idiocy of rural life," were subscribed to by the supposedly moderate leaders of the Second International. It is this radical noncapitalism that Marx understood as the "rational" organization of society and the end of history. Hence Lenin was quite orthodox in his obsession that "small [peasant] production gives birth to capitalism and the bourgeoisie continuously, daily, hourly, spontaneously."

In the period 1848–1881 a revolutionary movement at last emerged in Russia that is usually treated as something quite separate from Western radicalism. First, Russian revolutionary socialism, or populism, looked to the peasantry and its village commune rather than to the proletariat as the basis for a new society in Russia. Second, populism practiced terrorism whereas Western radicals placed their faith in the logic of history. But these distinctions accord too much importance to formal programs and tactics. In fact, both the Russian and the Western revolutionary movements are cognate expressions of the same wave of leveling democracy that had been moving across Europe since 1830. There are differences, of course. In preindustrial Russia radical intellectuals had no choice but to take the peasants as their universal class; since it is almost impossible to seize state power with a peasantry, these intellectuals fell back on terrorism. By contrast, an urban working class, as Lenin later demonstrated, is a much better vehicle for seizing political power. Yet when this working class is weak, it too can turn to anarchist terrorism and violent syndicalism, as the Western record at the turn of the century indicates. But the chief equalizer between Eastern and Western radicalism is that both the proletariat and the peasantry are completely utopian bases for socialism, whose chances everywhere rest with intellectuals.

The Russian revolutionary movement began in the 1840s at the same time as its German counterpart; Aleksandr Herzen and Bakunin discovered the peasant commune only shortly after Marx discovered the proletariat. From that time on, the Russian and Western movements evolved in tandem. The first translation of *Capital*, in 1872, was into Russian. In the late 1870s, the populists of the Will of the People looked to Marx as their mentor. He in turn was so impressed by these terrorists—after the Paris Commune's failure in 1871 the only going revolutionary movement in Europe—that he half bought into their populist utopia. As he wrote the year before his death in the preface to the first Russian translation of the *Manifesto:*

"If the Russian Revolution becomes the signal for the proletarian revolution in the West, so they both complement each
other, the present Russian common ownership of land may
serve as the starting point of a Communist development."
Once again, he edged toward the idea of telescoped revolution,
this time with direct reference to Russia. Shortly after his
death Petr Lavrov and Georgii Plekhanov represented Russia
at the founding congress of the Second International.

THE CONTRADICTIONS OF MARXISM

Created on the hundreth anniversary of the French Revolution, this body was much more impressive than its predecessor. Not only did it have a common body of doctrine in Engels's "positivistic" Marxism, but it federated real socialist
parties in the major European countries. For modern industry,
as yet feebly developed and confined to England and France
before 1848, had now spread across Europe as far east as the
Russian Empire. Accordingly, the new socialist parties soon
were flanked with strong trade unions. At the same time, socialism at last came to play an active political role through the
progress of parliamentary democracy. Only an experiment in
1792, and again a failure in 1848, universal suffrage was dura
bly adopted in France in 1870; something approximating it was
enacted in England in 1884; and Bismarck granted it to the
lower, and weaker, house of the new German parliament in
1871.

The right of worker association and universal suffrage,
considered radical in the first half of the century, at its end
proved to be conservative, or at least stabilizing, devices that
at last brought out the internal contradiction of Marxism. By
the century's end it had become apparent that capitalism was
not breaking down under the pressure of industrial concentra-

tion; on the contrary, the economy was expanding and the workers' lot was improving. And the workers, far from developing a revolutionary consciousness, were becoming reformist. So at the end of the 1890s Eduard Bernstein declared Marx to be wrong in his basic predictions. In answer, the party majority under Kautsky condemned this "revisionism" as the evisceration of Marxism—which indeed it was—and vehemently reaffirmed traditional orthodoxy. It did so, however, with an unavowed revisionism of its own: the theory that socialism could triumph by achieving a parliamentary majority—a "revolutionary waiting," as Kautsky called it, as utopian in its way as Marx's big red bang.

In this crisis of Marx's Marxism, it is the thirty-two-year-old Lenin who in 1902 produced the "workable" way out. He basically agreed with Bernstein's assessment of the workers' trade union aspirations but was horrified by his reformist conclusions. For he saw that Russia, unlike the Reich, was entering a revolutionary crisis reminiscent of Germany's revolt against its Old Regime in 1848. At the same time, unlike imperial Germany, pre-1905 Russia offered no semiconstitution and trade unions to moderate the radical drive. Hence, like Marx in 1848, Lenin dreamed that the proletariat could spearhead the impending revolt. Yet given the workers' trade union "consciousness," he concluded that revolutionary consciousness must be brought to them "from without" by members of the "bourgeois intelligentsia" who possessed "scientific knowledge" of history's purpose and its revolutionary laws. In other words, a "vanguard party" of professional revolutionaries would have to lead the proletariat in the coming revolution. Lenin's theory of the vanguard party in reality supplied the hitherto missing link in Marx's doctrine. Yet the germ of Lenin's theory of the intelligentsia as revolutionary avant-garde is clearly present in Marx's *Manifesto:*

> The Communists, therefore, are on the one hand, practically, the most advanced and resolute section of the working class parties of every country, that section which pushes forward all others; on the other hand, theoretically, they have *over the great mass of the proletariat the advantage of clearly understanding the line of march, the conditions, and ultimate general results of the proletariat movement* (emphasis added).

To this may be added that Marx directed the First International in proto-Leninist fashion, manipulating, splitting, and eventually scuttling this "workers" organization rather than have it taken over by the wrong ideology, that is, Bakunin's anarchism.

It is necessary to insist on the Marxist roots of Leninism because they have been so consistently denied. Beginning with the Mensheviks and Kautsky, Lenin's October has been condemned as a betrayal of Marxism and a reversion to the specifically Russian and conspiratorial tradition of the Will of the People. Yet, though the program of the Will of the People was peasant oriented, its organizational form was not specifically Russian; it was a replica of the secret societies of the pre-1848 West, of which the Communist League, for which Marx wrote his *Manifesto*, was one. Moreover, the organizational form of the Russian Socialist Democratic Party, as of its Bolshevik faction, was borrowed from the German SD party, not the Will of the People. The latter was a conspiracy of two hundred members, with no mass base; bolshevism was a conspiracy with an imperative need for a mass base, both in opposition and in power, and the SD hierarchical structure provided the framework for such broad mobilization.

Above all, however, it is passing strange in assessing Lenin to argue that a man who all his life swore by Marx, and whose every move was justified with Marxist categories, was really

not a Marxist but a crypto-populist. This can be done only by
reducing Marxism to one of its components, the logic of history. But this is to miss the dynamic of Marxism as a whole,
and hence to fail to understand the extraordinary attraction-
repulsion exercised by communism throughout the twentieth
century.

In fact, the real answer to the false problem of Lenin's orthodoxy is that Marxism presents to all its practitioners an
intrinsically *impossible* task. For the lockstep logic of history
does not mesh with the system's motive force, revolutionary
consciousness and the class struggle. No matter how "mature" capitalism becomes—anywhere, anytime—the schizo-
phrenic Marxist fantasy can never be realized in its entirety.
So its adepts have to choose one or the other of its basic components. Bernstein (and de facto Kautsky) chose waiting out
history's logic and so never reached socialism as noncapitalism. Lenin chose the primacy of "scientific revolutionary consciousness," and so made the only "proletarian" revolution
the world has ever known. Surely, this Bolshevik was not the
disciple who departed the farthest from Marx or betrayed his
millenial faith.

THE MILLENARIAN DELUSION

It is precisely that faith that produced the communist disaster and the eventual Soviet collapse, for the faith was a millenarian delusion that led, not to the end of history but to a
society more oppresive than the one it sought to transcend.

The disaster began when Lenin and Trotsky in October
1917 acted on an approximation of Marx's scenario for Germany in 1848, using the proletariat as a springboard to power
in Russia in the expectation that their bold deed would trigger
a European revolution. Yet, while awaiting that deliverance,

the party, as the incarnate stand-in for the proletariat, responded to the continuing "class struggle" within Russia by expropriating the "bourgeoisie," including its small peasant elements, and so found itself attempting a precocious "transition to communism." In its ardor it became convinced that this effort would, at the least, serve as a model for the future, as the Paris Commune had, or, at best, mark the beginning of real socialism in Russia.

But, of course, the Western revolution did not occur. Yet this failure did not shake the party's faith, for it could be rationalized on the grounds that, by capitalism's very nature, such a "stabilization" would be only temporary; in the meantime the party's duty to the world proletariat was to hold the fort in Russia. Even so, the party now found itself perilously isolated in a backward peasant country, confronted with a hostile population and an economy ruined by civil war, and, above all, by its own experiment in "building socialism."

So in 1921 the party, in order to survive in power, beat a partial retreat to "capitalism" by accepting a quasi-market in agriculture and small commerce while retaining control of the economy's "commanding heights" in heavy industry and credit. This New Economic Policy (NEP) for a time was rationalized by Nikolai Burkharin as "growing into socialism through the market." Still, contrary to widespread assumption, recourse to the market by Bukharin was only a temporary expedient, and the socialism he had in mind remained the full noncapitalism of the *Manifesto* and the Bolshevik party program.

In fact, the NEP turned out to be only a "breathing space." By 1928 it had enabled the country to revive sufficiently to make possible another leap into utopia, and in 1929–1934 this new socialist offensive was carried through to victory by Stalin. Casting himself as the "Lenin of today" and his first Five-

Year Plan as a "Second October," he plunged the country into an unprecedentedly brutal campaign of crash industrialization and the total collectivization of agriculture. By the middecade this revolution from above had abolished for the first time in history private property, profit, and the market and replaced them with a single "rational" plan. After having thus "built socialism," in 1936–1938 the leader purged the party so thoroughly of all who doubted the wisdom of his course that by the decade's end he presided over a virtually new organization. All its members were products and accomplices of the new system and hence wedded to its future fate. It is these cadres who would carry "real socialism" forward until the time of its collapse in the 1980s.

At this point democratic socialists, or simply common-sense observers, will object that Stalinist totalitarianism represents a complete departure from real Marxism, which was after all as much about "human emancipation" as about the logic of history. In this view, although Lenin, Trotsky, and Bukharin may be regarded as honest fanatics, Stalin must be considered a power-hungry cynic or a paranoid psychopath or a Russian nationalist. Such explanations are indeed partially valid. But to insist on them unduly is to forget that he was first of all "Lenin's faithful disciple"; that he took the party's "ideological work" so seriously that he himself wrote the chapter on dialectical materialsm for the *Short Course* of 1938, communism's breviary for decades to come; and that in private he referred to collectivization as "the cause." Hence when he represented the party's revolution from above against "petty bourgeois, capitalist kulaks" as a "class struggle" that grew more ferocious the nearer one got to socialism, we had better believe he believed it. For to him, socialism was above all the "highest" form of state building.

The dialectic of Stalinism is indeed surreal, but it is not

meaningless. It is rather the highest form of that inversion of reality that results when one attempts to implement the impossible. Thus, with Stalin, the Promethean Marxist program of permanent revolution in a situation of backwardedness led to the upside-down result of an ideological Leninist vanguard producing by coercion from above the industrial and proletarian society that was supposed to have created it by historical logic from below. Stalin's heirs continued in this ideocratic vein, waging the cold war as an "international class struggle" almost until the end of Sovietism.

It is this same inverted nature of communist reality that explains its brusque collapse. For the "command-administrative" methods of communist pseudo-modernization are not a rational plan at all but simply crude military methods applied to economic and social problems. As such, they were good only for a rapid breakthrough to an imitative industrialization in the 1930s or for national mobilization during the Second World War or for crash nuclear and ballistic development after it. But over the long haul such methods are an inhibiting factor for modernization in the fullest sense of the word. Hence, in the postwar era, as the "capitalist" world grew richer, it became apparent that the socialist world was falling into archaic stagnation; as the regime opened up a bit to the West in the 1960s and the 1970s, the Soviet elites increasingly saw the difference.

Consequently, since the whole point of socialism is to be "higher" than capitalism, the elites lost faith in the system's legitimating ideology. Whereas the generation of Leonid Brezhnev and Mikhail Suslov believed in the ideology down to its disappearance in the 1980s, the generation of Aleksandr Yakovlev and Mikhail Gorbachev was ridden with doubt; cadres more junior still knew that the system was simply a "lie," in Solzhenitsyn's term. And so, when Gorbachev tried to revive it with the semitruth of glasnost, the ideology simply evaporated into thin air—and with it all the allegedly "irreversible conquests" of socialism. For without ideology there were no longer any "class warriors" to defend the system; there was only a *nomenklatura* willing to settle for privatizing its rubble.

THE PATTERNS OF FAILURE

Thus, 150 years after the *Communist Manifesto*, and a century after the revisionist controversy, the perverse fate of Marxism had worked itself out fully. Since the two axes of the theory—historical necessity and the revolutionary consciousness of the proletariat—never intersected in the real world, we have two patterns of failure.

On the one hand, as Bernstein well understood, the "logic" of industrial society did not lead to communism but to a prosaic welfare state brokered by the power of universal suffrage (this is also where the orthodox Kautsky wound up). This outcome is hardly to be scorned, but Marxism is not necessary to achieve it; reformist and gradualist Fabianism or a mere New Deal can do as well. Indeed, completely nonsocialist movements have had just as much to do with it. The world's first draft of the welfare state was authored by the arch-conservative Bismarck in the 1880s. In post–World War II Italy and Germany, Christian Democrats had more to do with it than Social Democrats. Indeed, *horrible dictu* Mussolini and Hitler built more comprehensive welfare states in the 1930s than did Franklin Roosevelt, not to mention Britain's Stanley Baldwin, who came up with nothing better than the dole. In short, whatever the triggering ideology, the welfare state is simply part of any viable "capitalist" modernity.

On the other hand, as was demonstrated by Lenin's formula for forcing the two axes of Marxism together, the "proletarian revolution" can be carried to completion only by those professionals of revolutionary consciousness who stem from "the bourgeois intelligentsia." It is therefore quite logical that Marxism in practice produced results that were the opposite of what it predicted in theory, for only the violence of "class warfare" against the party's supposed social base could create the full noncapitalism of "real" socialism.

And so by 1991 the inevitable failure of this solution had destroyed Marxism and indeed the two-century-old socialist tradition in general. For it is now clear that in real history there no such thing as a "proletarian revolution." In fact, there is no such thing as a "bourgeois revolution," either; 1789 is best defined as the paradigmatic modern, or democratic, revolt against a traditional Old Regime. By the same token, there is no such thing as a "socialist society" waiting at the exit from capitalism; there is only a Soviet-type regime; and it is necessary to be Marxist to build such a surreal structure on the sufferings of others.

Thus the last two centuries of Western politics have been in thrall to the myth of a two-stage modernity, first "bourgeois," then "socialist." Whole regimes have been built on this illusion, and millions have been killed in its name. In fact, however, it is now clear that there is only one modernity, as defined by the universal suffrage republic, first sketched in 1793 and durably realized comprehensively in much of the West two or three decades before 1917.

Moreover, it is because the ultimate program of socialists and Social Democrats was akin to that of Communists that in 1989–1991 Western socialism collapsed along with Eastern communism. Thus, European socialist parties, after helping to build Europe's postwar welfare states, by the end of the century had nothing left to do. And so the world is left with the pressure of universal suffrage to keep pushing the venerable "bourgeois" republic to ever new phases of egalitarian politics, as matters have moved from class to race to gender.

Yet the question remains: Is the drive for the political millennium really dead? Or are we now living a utopian capitalism in the guise of globalization? And might not the as yet unknown crises of our current end of history bring a return of utopian politics?

It is for this reason also that socialism and social democracy quietly followed communism into oblivion after 1989–1991; for the *schism* between the two lefts created by October was always less absolute than is generally supposed. Although with time Social Democrats recognized that Bernstein's diagnosis of Marxism was accurate, they retained Kautsky's orthodox program until well after the Second World War; and that program proposed the same full noncapitalism as Marx—or Lenin. The German SDs renounced it only in 1969, Francois Mitterrand *half* attempted a "transition to socialism" in 1981, and British Labour did not abandon its "point four" of full nationalization until 1997. It was thus only the collapse of the Soviet version of their own ultimate program that definitively killed the socialists' aspirations to someday "transcend" capitalism. And so, after helping to create the postwar welfare state, they are now commited to privatization and market liberalism.

Yet does this outcome mean that longing for an egalitarian end of history is at last dead? Or might the invisible hand of globalization inadvertently revise it in some new form? The impending calendar millennium will surely have this matter high on its agenda.

6

The Silent Artillery
of Communism

Michael Novak

FOR SEVENTY-TWO YEARS, communism in Russia waged a silent war against the human soul. Sometimes screams were heard from torture chambers deep in prisons and in detention centers, but, mostly, the war was fought with ideas and incessant public propaganda. Below the surface, it eroded foundations. Out of sight, it taught people to have a low opinion of themselves, as if they were incapable of nobility of soul. It ridiculed the soul's capacity for discernment and for truth. Year after year, its silent artillery leveled the inner landscapes of the soul.

My aim, after certain introductory remarks, is to pull two forgotten themes from the rubble of the fall of communism. The collapse of communism in 1989 was one of the greatest events of human history—sudden, unexpected (although Wojtyla was not surprised), dramatic, and utterly transformative. We are too close to it to be certain how to read it. Yet one characteristic of communism proved to be decisive, but easy to overlook. I mean its particular form of atheism and the long-term effect of this atheism on the morale of the people and their economic performance. These last two themes reward attention: atheism's effect on the soul and on economic vitality.

ON HUMAN CAPITAL

A more secular way to speak of these things is to say that communism set out to destroy human capital. It set out, for instance, to eradicate centuries of learning, habits, cultures— to erase what it chose to call "bourgeois culture" and to salt it as Carthage was salted and to plow it under and even to pour oceans of sludge on top of it: lies, propaganda, agitprop. In the process, in one generation, and then in two, and three, and almost four, communism destroyed the simple habits of economic life. It wounded enterprise, investment, innovation, even the ability to distinguish between profit and loss (since in the end the state didn't care, and paid whatever it wished to pay). It wounded, as well, simple habits of honesty and trust, self-reliance and the honor of being faithful to one's word. More deeply still, it dulled the most distinctive human mark: the soul's primordial endowment of creativity, its sense of personal responsibility, its knowledge of itself as a *subject*.

I need to linger on this last point a moment. The denial of the dignity of the individual, the reduction of the human being to merely material elements, erases the awareness humans have of themselves as persons who reflect and who choose, who launch new and creative actions into history, and who accept responsibility for their actions. Not to be misunderstood, this is the meaning I attach to *subject*. Unlike a horse or a cow, a human being is an acting person, an active agent—

inquiring and understanding, deliberating, judging, deciding. In precisely these ways, a human is made in the image of God. Therein lies both his unparalleled glory and the probability of his tragic and often bitter falls.

Communism aimed to objectify everything and everybody. Its fundamental premise was materialism. Human beings are . . . meat. Animated for a time, perhaps, but essentially no more than a *sachetto* of chemicals. Instruments. Means. The "dialectical" part of "dialectical materialism" belonged to a dynamic class position. The "materialist" part describes human beings. (Truly, it is hard to believe that anybody really believed this, but some did.) The individual should *expect* to be expended, sacrificed, used up, like a thing. Like the steel girders he could see rusting, unwanted and unused, outside the mills of Nowa Huta.

Sacrificed—in this last respect, communism traded on deep symbolic resonances emanating from Judaism and Christianity. Among these are the long expectation of a New Jerusalem, and the sacrifice of self for others like the ritual lamb, or in the image of the Savior. Communism's materialistic theory, in and of itself, had no such resonance. Mere things do not make sacrifices for noble purposes. Mere things do not consider sacrifice a noble act. Communism's deepest sentiments were borrowed.

THE *VIA NEGATIVA*

It is well known that belief in God can lead to torture, as in the awful scrutinies of heresy tribunals. It is less well known that atheism of a particular kind also leads to torture. The two routes to torture are quite different. The temptation of believers comes from moral arrogance or its mirror image, as in the case of Dostoevsky's Grand Inquisitor, who was moved to torture by "pity," a foolish belief that most people are not as wise as he, so that it was his "duty" to keep them from liberty. This route begins in moral debility. With atheists of the communist kind it is quite different. Here torture flows from its fundamental premises about the human being. No human has any worth apart from contributing to the Cause, to the Dialectic, to the triumph of the Party (the Vanguard of History, the Custodian of human fate). If a man will not contribute willingly to History or (it comes to the same thing) the Collective Will of the Party, he is without value and may be disposed of—indeed, may be a threat to the Party and *should* be disposed of. Still, though, some utility may be squeezed from him. If necessary, squeeze.

The bile that rises to our mouths when we contemplate the record of believers who administered torture or committed devout dissenters to the flames is informed by our belief that they were hypocrites, profoundly betraying the example of their Teacher and all His deeper lessons. They were traitors, hypocrites, betrayers, the more to be despised because the level of the teaching they purported to protect was so high. Importuned to be meek and humble, they were arrogant and swollen mightily with pride until their eyes were blinded to the horror of their deeds. One thinks, "They ought, at least, to have been faithful to the faith that they professed." *They deserve to be condemned in the light of their own beliefs*, because those beliefs did *not* lead logically to the torturing of others, quite the opposite. Such men snaked circuitously to that place, held close to the earth by pride.

The case was altogether different with the Communists. Some of them, of course, never really believed their philosophical indoctrination. For various motives, however, good party members *acted them out*. Against Communists who are torturers, one cannot appeal to the figure of Christ or to the commandments of God. One cannot appeal to natural law or moral law or "bourgeois illusions." They have their orders. History has a certain logic. They can be quite well trusted to overcome their own feelings and do what is required to turn a man into a means for the party's ends. Their feelings, also, can be trained, as can their minds. What is an individual man, after all?

Countless memoirs from survivors tell us in detail the logic of the Gulag and how it worked. We have the testimony of Andrei Sakharov and of Anatole Scharansky. We have the memoirs of Mihailo Mihailov and Armando Valladares. We have Arthur Koestler's *Darkness at Noon*. We have scores of thousands of windswept camps, millions of graves. Not the mechanics, not even the "logic," but rather the underlying vision of the human being interests us now.

I am certain that I have read more eloquent literary statements than the following. But for clarity and economy of speech I have encountered nothing equal to it:

> The fundamental error of socialism is anthropological in nature. Socialism considers the individual person simply as an element, a molecule within the social organism, so that the good of the individual is completely subordinated to the functioning of the socio-economic mechanism. Socialism likewise maintains that the good of the individual can be realized without reference to his free choice, to the unique and exclusive responsibility which he exercises in the face of good or evil. Man is thus reduced to a series of social relationships, and the concept of the person as the autonomous subject of moral decision disappears, the very subject whose decisions build the social order.
>
> From this mistaken conception of the person there arise both a distortion of law, which defines the sphere of the exercise of freedom, and an opposition to private property. A person who is deprived of something he can call "his own,"

and of the possibility of earning a living through his own
initiative, comes to depend on the social machine and on
those who control it. This makes it much more difficult for
him to recognize his dignity as a person, and hinders progress
towards the building up of an authentic human community.

This text, of course, is from *Centesimus Annus* (para. 13).
Here Wojtyla does something quite unusual for a pope; he em-
ploys an encyclical, a formal tool designed for teaching the
Gospel to the entire circle of nations (hence *encyclical*), for the
purpose of interpreting one single historical event; the whole
of its second chapter is given to the meaning and causes of the
extraordinary year 1989. *Centesimus Annus* is an astonishing
encyclical. It is much too neglected in Europe.

The pope's point is philosophical; one does not have to be
a believer to grasp it. If at the core of man's being nothing
"calls" him in a way that demands a response—a free and un-
coerced exercise of his personal responsibility, in the secret
depths of his heart—then the "dignity" attributed to him for
some centuries now is without reality. That call to "respond"
engenders *responsibility*, which in the vastness of these gal-
axies grounds our dignity.

Certain types of Western atheists have an analogous point
of view. They also recognize human responsibility—to truth,
to reality, perhaps to justice, and even to love. It is just that
they lack the talent for, the gift of, recognizing God. When
they look, they "see" nothing there. Yet as they do not believe
in God, nor do they believe that human liberty is just a neural
reflex. They have known in themselves a willing exercise of
reflection, deliberation, and the sort of choice that is a commitment, on which others can count. They are atheists for
whom "truth," "honor," and "courage" are not empty words.
(I myself have met many such. As readers of *Belief and Unbe-*

lief and *The Experience of Nothingness* will know, I have sometimes wondered why I should not include myself among them.)

For one reason or another, such men and women cannot bring themselves, even when they try, to be at peace in accepting belief in God; they simply do not see. To the extent that they are atheists, so far as they are aware, this is because they are not internally compelled by evidence to the contrary. (Sometimes, they confess, there are hidden desires impeding their will to see, which they have not the inclination to override.) In most other crucial human respects, they share with the theist a sense of a transcendent order that is not made by man, but to which a man can only respond as honestly and courageously as he (or she) knows how. As I once wrote:

> Atheists who are not nihilists know that they are bound by conscience, which they find in their own reason and in the judgment of their fellows down the ages. And if despite their beliefs, there is a God, they expect that reason is in accord with the judgment of God. No one escapes.

The fact that there are many such atheists led me to speak above of "the particular kind" of atheism found in communism, which, by contrast, denies any transcendent dimension to being, any "call" to which humans must freely respond, any standard of truth, evidence, moral integrity, and goodness by which humans are every moment being judged. For the Communist, all is nothingness except the Dialectic of History, before which and in whose name he prostrates himself. The Communist borrows from Christians and Jews an improper comfort, namely, that his prostration places him on the side of an idealistic justice and compassion for workers in which his premises forbid him to believe. Respecting moral principles, he can have only one: the Collective Will of the Party. All else can be done in that name: murder, torture, imprison, exterminate, assassinate. No other moral question can be scientifically raised. Respecting moral comfort, the Communist is a thief.

For communism, there is in man no internal source of dignity. Personal liberty and personal responsibility cannot be honored in theory, although of course they continued to live on. In theory, these realities were dismissed as bourgeois affectations.

Paradoxically, the communist system of imprisonment, torture, and public confession constituted, despite itself, a *via negativa* that led a great many of its victims to God, and to a fresh sense of being an *individual* who possesses *dignity*. For under torture they discovered evidence for the presence of God at the core of their own being. The prison literature of our time is full of such instances.

The typical pattern, if I am not mistaken, went like this. The KGB handbooks listed more than twenty different degrees of torture, more or less scientifically studied and refined. At some point in the proceedings, the torturer would tell his victim that there is no point in resisting, why put everybody through the pain? "No one will ever know what happens here. It has no significance. Neither resistance nor confession, really, will affect the outcome of History. Just be pragmatic. Tell me what I wish, write what I request, and do it sooner rather than later. Why not? Bourgeois prejudices? You are too intelligent for that. No one is ever going to know what you or I will do here. It will be locked up in files with millions of others files, and a thousand years from now when socialism is truly consolidated, people will never even notice. Consider yourself a forgotten man. Be practical. Sign now rather than later. There is no such thing as truth. It is only a matter of making a decision. It is a matter of will. Write down what you know is fact. I will even help you. The sooner I can go home the better for me—and for you. It is a matter of will. Be practical."

And then the light would go on in the victim's head. "My torturer is telling me that he has all the power. But he is actually confessing something else. There is something he wants from me that he does not have. So he does not have *all* the power. What he needs is this: that I should conform. He needs my will. He needs my denial that there is any such thing as truth. Only then will his philosophy be confirmed.

"As long as I remain faithful to my own intellect and will, as long as I refuse to be complicit in his lie, then my existence unsettles him. *I will not tell a lie.* As long as I can hold out for that principle, then my existence shows him that his philosophy is false.

"Of course, he will overpower me. He can break me with pain. He can take away my mind and my liberty with drugs. But the real power in this relationship is mine. He cannot get what he wants unless I freely give it to him. It is not enough for him to force me, to destroy me—that would be only an instant's work. I am totally in his power. Except for the sanctuary of my consciousness, my fidelity to the light. He will strip me of everything but honesty and naked will. These I cannot give him. He will have to destroy me, and then he cannot have them. Death is now my friend. I will be no use to him—or his precious party—dead."

Along this way, very much like the way that St. John of the Cross marked out in *The Dark Night of the Soul*, thousands of victims came to know themselves at a depth they had never experienced before. They began to distinguish among the movements of their own souls memory, imagination, desire, dread, understanding, will.

Moreover, when their bodies ached with pain from beatings, and from the application of electrical current, and from being contorted and held for hours in positions of excruciating pain, they learned something else. They learned that the light inside themselves, to which they were trying to be faithful, the light of truth (or at least the will not to be complicit in any lie), cannot properly be said to be *part of themselves*. That was, of course, their first awareness, that they were being faithful to themselves, clinging to their own minds and wills. When the pain becomes intense enough, however, one sees that one is not really suffering this for oneself. If that were so, why would one not just surrender and make the pain go away? Why wouldn't one be pragmatic?

Rather, it certainly seemed as though, in being faithful to the truth and in calling up his stubborn courage of will, a man was answering to something that did not belong to himself, something that called (although it had no voice) from outside his own mind and will, something at any rate not reducible to his own mind. His own mind and will were focused in a direction running contrary to everything good for his body and his comfort and his peace. But why? Why was he running from his own self-interest, narrowly considered?

On the matter of self-interest, his torturer was certainly correct. In fact, the torturer's insistence on self-interest suggested the one line of thought that explained why the torturer was wrong.

The light in my mind (before which I am trying to be honest) is, as it were, something I *participate* in, and it is not reducible to me. This light approves of my liberty and grows brighter with my own acts of responsibility to it. This light seems very like what people mean—the people an atheist couldn't earlier understand—when they speak of God. And yet (as St. John of the Cross insists) in the place where we would like God to be, "no one appears." Only silence. Emptiness. Nothingness. Yet from emptiness strength emanates, and from it one feels constantly stronger. And more comforted, despite the wracking pain and weariness and tedium, than by anything one has ever before experienced. And one feels *true*.

I did my best to express this in my Templeton Address:

> To obey truth is to be free, and in certain extremities nothing is more clear to the tormented mind, nothing more vital to the survival of self-respect, nothing so important to one's sense of remaining a worthy human being—of being no one's cog, part of no one's machine, and resister to death against the kingdom of lies—nothing is so dear as to hold to truth. In fidelity to truth lies human dignity.
>
> There is nothing recondite in this. Simple people have often seen it more clearly than clerks.

This is the plain insight that Aleksandr Solzhenitsyn expressed, as did Silvester Krcmery—a man who may have endured solitary confinement, without breaking, longer than any living man—in his magnificent memoir, *Breakpoint* (Herder and Herder, 1999).

TO THE THRESHOLD

In the *via negativa*, the voyager sees nothing, hears no divine voices, feels no mystic "presence." As it were, he has before him no more "evidence" concerning God than he did when he called himself an atheist. But he can no longer call himself that. He has come to know that he is no longer accurately described as an atheist. He has been led to the threshold where God dwells by a dark and obscure knowledge that carries with it a warrant unmistakable to those who have participated in it. He may or may not be ready to say that he believes in "God," but now he has had the experiences that allow him to know what others have been talking about. Not that these are "experiences" that can be isolated, or that they are a kind of "special knowledge" given to some but not to others. Rather, something much more simple.

In the act of fidelity to the light—the resolve not to be willingly complicit in any lie—a man has become aware of a dimension of his being he had never glimpsed before in such stark clarity. In this awareness, he is aware of a powerful personal dignity. What impresses him is its inalienability. Unless he is simply destroyed, it cannot be taken away from him without his consent. It is true that later he may weaken and give in. But he does not have to fight *later*, only now. He needs only to concentrate during this staccato second, one second at a time, on the dark light within. Silvester Krcmery simply concentrated on repeating the words of the Gospel of St. John, the whole of which he had committed to memory. Too broken sometimes to think of *meanings*, he found even the effort to recite the mere words nourishing. And, of course, the meanings when he had strength to grasp them illuminated what he was enduring.

The term *dignus* is a precious term in the vocabulary of the West. That single word helps to explain why we attach so much importance to the millennium—rather, the *second* millennium. For it was Jesus Christ, bringing the Torah to the Gentiles, who taught humankind that Plato was wrong to teach that the lowly have slavish souls, souls of lead, whereas their superiors have souls of gold and silver. Even the children, even the poor, even the outcasts, every one of God's children, Jesus said, as the Torah also taught through the prophets, is *dignus*. The world has never been the same.

That term attaches great worth, nobility, immortal and incommensurable value to every woman and every man, each of whose names, the Pentateuch tells us, the Creator knows and calls. The Bible assigns humans this status as *dignus*, as it does to no other creature, for reasons that, strictly, we do not need revelation to reveal: our capacity for ordered liberty, for the exercise of responsibility, for living in the truth. That term *dignus* made possible the rise of modern science, by raising even the poor in their own estimation, and calling upon their enormous, hidden talents, and instructing all humans that fidelity to truth is in touch with the way things are, and giving all the vocation to inquire in the light of truth. Fidelity to truth is a way of participating in the life of God. Truth and Light are among the names God gives Himself in the biblical record.

In a way too little reflected upon, Wojtyla the philosopher has articulated a crucial point: the close relation between atheism and the disappearance of individual dignity, and between theism and the inner experience of dignity. But, I hasten to add again, "atheists" of fidelity to truth and goodwill have also experienced their own dignity in acts of responsibility and reflective liberty. As Albert Camus once wrote, there are atheists in our time who lack nothing but churchgoing to distinguish them from believers. In *Belief and Unbelief*, I show how in the darkness the inner life of both the serious believer and the serious unbeliever can be quite similar, except that for the believer perhaps it can be less comforting. The atheist, after all, says he expects the darkness.

To that last point, however, honesty forces me to add that for Jews and Christians, truth is not merely a property of propositions or even a term for fidelity to the light. It is a personal name, the name of a Person. So that participation in fidelity to truth is, in the eyes of faith, communion with a Beloved. But to say this much takes us beyond the *via negativa*. I will say no more than that faith does not take away the experience of emptiness, of *nada*. Clouds of witnesses have so testified.

Let me return speedily, therefore, to the first part of my argument. This anniversary of the fall of communism forces us to confront one of the deepest lessons to be gleaned from a

seventy-year plague upon the human race. Even in the emptiness, the sheer willingness not to turn away from the light, not
to be complicit in a lie, leads to an experience of the emptiness
in which God darkly dwells. Receptivity is all. It is as though
our inquiring souls are already God-shaped. Silently formed in
His image. So that when we try to be honest and brave, try to
hold a steady light, that obscure light is already a form of participation.

For seventy-two years, communism leveled its silent artillery on this image in the human soul. Its aim was to level the
soul's grandeur, to make it more pliable as an instrument of
the Collective Will. In such a system, torture is not an accident. Torture expresses its essence: The human individual has
no worth.

And yet, ironically, the experience of this torture upon
their own flesh led many thousands of ordinary people to an
extraordinary recovery. In the recesses of their own being, they
witnessed the hidden action of God. By this *via negativa*,
those determined to cleanse the world of God were divinely
outmaneuvered. Trying to drive God out of the soul, they tor-
mented the soul into abandoning everything else, there by negation to find Him.

THE DESTRUCTION OF HUMAN CAPITAL

Before communism collapsed in 1989, it had also lowered
its silent artillery on the human capital of its people, especially
the human capital that suited them for personal economic initiative. (Communism forbade capitalist acts between con-
senting adults, in some circumstances under penalty of death.)
In defining the nature of capitalism, however, Karl Marx made
an egregious mistake. He thought that capitalism is constituted by three institutional arrangements: (1) private property,

(2) a market system of exchange, and (3) the private accumulation of profit. These three institutions, however, are all *pre*-capitalist. They are found even in the biblical period (and earlier), whereas scholars hold that "capitalism" is something very new, modern in fact and quite different from the traditional system based on private property, markets, and profit. Max Weber dated the birth of capitalism after the Protestant Reformation (also a mistake, but indicative of the timing). During the years after 1775, Adam Smith, David Hume, and others in Scotland and England were arguing for a *new* system, a system that did not yet exist except *in nuce*. They made, as O. E. Hirshman puts it, "arguments for capitalism before its arrival."

The defining dynamic of the new system is *invention* and *enterprise*. Capitalism applied imagination and practical intelligence to creating new goods and services not provided by earlier systems—agrarian, feudal, and mercantile. Adam Smith opened his *Inquiry into the Nature and Cause of the Wealth of Nations* (1776) with a description of the invention of the pin machine that made it possible to produce thousands of pins with less labor and expense than it had earlier cost to produce a dozen pins. Before, only duchesses could afford pins; afterward, every poor girl in the kingdom had them. In the nineteenth century, the real income of the poor in England rose by 1,600 percent.

In the United States in 1787, the U.S. Constitution included an article granting to "authors and inventors" for a limited time the right to the profits from their own inventions, in other words, *constitutional* protection for patents and copyrights. In the penetrating words of Abraham Lincoln not quite a century later, this patent system "added the fuel of interest to the fire of genius." Like a spark, this law changed the social position and meaning of wealth, for it shifted the focus of the pursuit of wealth off *land* and placed it on *enterprise,* invention, and discovery, away from the physical and material, and toward ideas. It took the focus of the will to power, that ineradicable fact of human life after the Fall, away from the generals and national glory and wooed it toward those who could create new wealth and international connectedness (now called globalization). What had three thousand years of generals and national glory done to raise the condition of the poor? David Hume asked. Only the spread of manufacturing and commerce could do that. *Commercium et Pax* was the wise motto of Amsterdam.

So it happens that nearly all business corporations (and even unincorporated businesses) in the United States today are based on creative ideas for new goods and services or new ways of providing them. The virtue of *enterprise,* in short, is the essence of capitalism; enterprise is the new dynamic in the world. Until enterprise is present in sufficient density, capitalism cannot even begin. In Poland in 1990, for example, after laws were reestablished protecting private property, restoring the market system of exchange, and allowing for the private creation of wealth, the question remained, Had the Polish people lost all habits of initiative under forty years of communist passivity? Would the new system simply die of inertia? As it happened, in the first six months of 1990, 500,000 new small businesses were formed. This spirit of enterprise provided lift-off. It has only grown stronger since.

In this respect Max Weber was correct (as against Marx)— that the explanatory factor in the new system lies in the realm of the spirit rather than in the material order. Capitalism is most of all a set of human habits—virtues, in the old-fashioned sense, natural and learned dispositions. For example, the virtue of enterprise consists, like the classical virtue of prudence, in both an intellectual habit and a moral habit. The intellectual habit is to *notice*, often before others do, new creative economic opportunities, new goods to create or new ways to create them, to *innovate*, to *invent*. The moral habit is to have the realism, the practicality, the know-how, and the stubborn obstinacy *to turn ideas into realities*; that is, *to make ideas work*. Not everybody who has one of these habits has the other. Enterprise requires both. Enterprise is not unlike the creative habit of the artist, who also makes to be what never was. People in business are not infrequently as vainglorious about their creations as any *diva* of the opera.

Thus, contrary to Max Weber, it is not precisely "hard work" or "asceticism" that creates new wealth, although both of those factors are highly supportive and almost always necessary. Rather, it is often the factor of serendipity, the gift of the act of creation, sometimes occurring suddenly in the ready mind as if inspired by a Muse, that ignites "the fire of invention." The creative act is what Rocco Buttiglione once called the "Don Quixote" factor.

The great sociologist Max Weber stressed what he called the "Protestant virtues," and I do not want to underestimate their importance. Actually, however, the *creativity* and élan of what I call the "Catholic virtues"—the zest for invention, a love for surprise and for wonder, and a sense that life is as much a gift as a result of hard work—are in actual practice closer to the mark. Creative people do not always work by schedules and routines. Thus, Northern Italy has been a creative precursor of capitalist activity for at least five centuries and today is one of the top ten entrepreneurial hot spots in the European Community. Catholics make too little of their own genius for enterprise. A political affection for social democracy among Catholics smothers this widely distributed genius; the long agrarian history of Catholicism predisposes many to "organic" theories, and dulls the vision of the capacity of enterprise to open opportunity to the poor. The British left shares this same bias, which Tony Blair's "Third Way" is meant to correct.

Contrary to Amintore Fanfani's famous book on capitalism, *Catholicism, Protestantism and Capitalism*, Catholic theology, freshly considered, throws a more illuminating light on the essence of capitalism than Max Weber and the "Protestant ethic" did and better explains the course of economic history. As David Landes of the Massachusetts Institute of Technology makes clear in his 1998 study of economic history, *The Wealth and Poverty of Nations*, one main cause of the economic leadership of the West lies in the "joy of discovery" taught to Jews and Christians, through the teaching that each woman and each man is made in the image of God, the Creator, and is called to be a creator too.

It goes without saying that communism tried to eradicate this image in the human soul and to strip away from society every social support that over the ages had been brought to its flourishing. Economic initiative was forbidden. The good socialist system was expected to be receptive to the collective will and to submerge individual creativity within it. Private property was abolished. (As late as 1986, along the banks of the dark river in the center of Moscow, huge red letters blazed at night: The Essence of Socialism Is the Abolition of Private Property.) The system of market exchange—as old as Jerusalem in the biblical period, for Jerusalem was nothing if not a marketplace at the crossroads of three continents—was replaced with a system of national planning. "Experts" had the task of setting prices each month for more than 20 million different items; they had to *fantasize* these "correct" prices, make them up out of whole cloth, *invent* them, with no reference to the costs, desires, or efforts expended by individual buyers or sellers; and they had to do so each month. The epistemic problem of knowing such things is beyond any team of mere mortals, as Ludwig von Mises had predicted in the 1920s. No wonder the socialist economy had a Mickey Mouse quality; epistemically, it had the realism of a comic strip.

As if that weren't bad enough, communism cut the tie between economic effort and reward. It forbade private accumulation and settled instead for rewarding its most faithful ones with political favors (including living quarters, dachas, automobiles, and "official" stores).

Not only this. Communism set out to abolish the ancient traditions, customs, and habits of law and morality. It wanted to dirty, distort, and bury the past so that it would be irrecoverable. It tried desperately to replace "bourgeois morality" (in reality, the morality of Judaism and Christianity, more dear to the poor perhaps than to the affluent) with "socialist morality," a morality of means and ends in which the human person is never an end but always a means. It taught disregard for critical thinking, personal judgment, and a love for truth in order to make room for Party ideology and propaganda.

As a final affront, it withheld even the humblest goods—toilet paper, meat, oranges—so that humble citizens would have to spend hours in line every week just in order to live. In this way, they might come to feel grateful for the smallest triumphs. They would also learn to hold themselves in contempt, as unworthy of anything at all except what was allotted them. Shortages demean people, and communism used them as a means of social control. (Those who too facilely oppose "being" to "having" have not reflected on the close relation, not only lexical, between the terms *proprius* and property and between the self and dominion over necessary and convenient things. Communism's war against the self traded on this distinction.)

Thus it is that, after seventy-two years of communist

"moral education," the legal and moral traditions of Russia are today in a shambles. The human capital built up over centuries of religious and humanistic striving was bleached out of each successive generation—one, two, three, four generations in all—and nothing was put in its place but cynicism. Means and ends. Instrumentalism.

In such a moral and legal environment, neither democracy nor capitalism can take root, let alone flourish. Democracy and capitalism are, both of them, sets of moral and intellectual habits before they are anything else—even before they are institutionalizations of these habits. "Democracy," Alexis de Tocqueville wrote, "is a long education." It is learned by experience and must be internalized. Like any fragile plant, however, it will grow only under a limited set of ecological conditions. There is an "ecology of liberty," as vital as the ecology of the biosphere—*more* vital. Communism tried for seventy-two years to raze that ecology, to plow it under, as the Romans plowed Carthage under: *Carthago delendum est.*

Few commentators have noticed this aspect of communist destructiveness. In destroying the heritage of religion and law, and in destroying the very idea of evidence-based truth (independent of preference or party, aimed squarely at an accurate assessment of reality), communism destroyed, or perhaps gravely injured, the "social capital" on which all human progress in liberty depends. The loss of social capital is an incalculable loss for individuals, for one person alone does not make a free society. Even if the ecology of liberty in a particular society is healthy, it takes a degree of heroism to act virtuously when others are not doing so. But when the whole ecology of the society frustrates your actions at every turn, trying to act virtuously in solitariness seems futile, and one must struggle daily against the temptation to despair. (This is perhaps why the pope keeps preaching "Be not afraid!" and why he lays so much stress on the desperate social need for hope, in our time especially.)

A metaphor for the communist destruction of human capital was suggested to me in the spring of 1990 by a brilliant priest in Prague, Tomaš Halík. Looking at the socialist skyline of Prague he said wryly: "Forty years of communism will be remembered for not one piece of worthy architecture. Look!" More than that, he pointed out to me that for forty years the Communists plowed not a korona back into capital maintenance of the existing buildings, except on a few Potemkin facades. The plumbing, wiring, and plaster were left as they had been in 1948, which meant in most cases as they had been in 1938, when the Nazis rolled into Prague. The Communists created little new capital and spent down the old. "It will take decades to bring these properties back to the condition in which the Communists confiscated them." Communism was like a tapeworm, devouring the capital, social, human, and even architectural, of its captive nations from within. One hears in Eastern Europe many wry jokes about this aspect of socialism.

In sum, communism was not merely an alternative to democracy and a dynamic, free economy. It destroyed the human capital on which a free economy and polity are based. It poisoned the ecology of liberty. Detoxifying it will require years of patient work in the moral and cultural sphere. Most Western economists, alas, have little or no comprehension of how much they take this sphere for granted.

THE WESTERN BLIND SPOT

Before concluding, let me tell a parable to exemplify this blind spot among Western economists, a parable I learned (and hereby adapt for present purposes) from an economist at

George Mason University, Jennifer Roback. She describes an American couple who adopted a young boy of three or so from Romania, one of those orphans brought up mass-production style, never held in human arms, fed by a bottle put in place by a mechanical apparatus. Isolated from human closeness with adults until he left the orphanage, the child is grown now, handsome, smart, winning in his ways—but absolutely incapable of forming a human relationship, only capable of seeking his own will and his own pleasure. He fears close contact with adults, only pretending to affection so far as is necessary. Cleverly narcissistic, he lies, steals, cheats, whatever he needs to do to obtain whatever he desires. And all the while, smiling, he charms people by his seemingly open manner. He has already been arrested once for shoplifting, and his teachers at school, for a time in love with him, have reluctantly had to report the times he has stolen things from his classmates.

This engaging boy has learned precisely how to deceive. His parents, serious and devout people, are in despair about his behavior. For he is certainly heading for self-destruction and may, they fear, charm innocent and inexperienced people into accompanying him thereto. Professor Roback explains that the totally self-centered impulse that moves this child, the total preoccupation with his own physical self-interest, at the expense of all other more noble interests (except insofar as pretending to these helps him to achieve his own purposes), sounds remarkably like what the economists conventionally discuss as "economic self-interest."

Professor Roback has even written a lecture to this effect, daring other economists to tell her in what respect the conduct of this warped and totally narcissistic (almost emotionally autistic) young man *differs* from the behavior of their theoretical "economic man." This challenge infuriates the economists, she has found, but they only sputter and do not answer it.

When they have had time to reflect upon it, however, they may find that, more than they recognize, *more than they explicitly recognize in their published theories,* the "man" they assume to be acting in their theories is a highly developed humanistic person, of Jewish and Christian provenance, or of some correlative tradition. For when they write "rational," they also mean "law-abiding" and at least minimally "honest," "trustworthy," and "morally reliable." They emphatically do *not* mean a crook, cheat, liar, manipulator, or narcissist with whom it is impossible to have a rational relationship. A deal has to be a deal. A partner one cannot trust brings a high cost in efficiency and a high probability of eventual disaster. The true anthropology of capitalism, the only premise on which it can work, encodes a far richer morality than is exemplified by that unfortunate orphan.

Analogously, an unfortunate orphan brought up until the age of three without human contact, warmth, or emotional involvement is not a fair metaphor for the ordinary people who endured the imposition of amoral communism upon them for seventy or (in Eastern Europe) forty years. But it *is* a fair metaphor for the aims and practices of communism. Our parable describes a human being rendered emotionally autistic by being treated as an object, raised like a little animal in a large stable (mechanically, without maternal embrace or touch), made over into a rational calculator of means and ends, evacuated of genuine and reliable *subjectivity.* Where there ought to be a "self" in him, there is a cipher. This child learned to determine his direction by vectoring around any resistance he meets to getting what he wants, like a robot bumping and bouncing away, incapable of internal self-government. Like the Eveready bunny, he never stops calculating and driving onward. Within his own personal history, there is a dialectic of resistant objects that have marked out the paths forced upon him: a kind of miniature Dialectical Materialism, blind and irresistible.

Also inhuman.

THE FREE SOCIETY

Long before World War II ended, a group of economists and philosophers in Germany began thinking about the *novus ordo* that would have to replace nazism, once Hitler came to the end of his line. They recognized that if they were to build a humane society they would have to reconstruct a new political order, a new economic order, and a new moral/cultural order. To construct any *one* of these orders is a herculean job, but to be obliged to construct all *three*—and to be obliged to do so almost simultaneously (although not instantaneously)— is virtually superhuman. The hope of these "*Ordo* economists," as they called themselves, was that Germany had not suffered total cultural and moral damage under nazism, given that the regime had lasted only twelve years. They further hoped that there were strong remnants of the humanistic past that could again be drawn on but in a more careful way. Their philosophy, and their vision of a "social market economy," became the practical guide to the "miraculous" success of Germany during the years 1945–1999. Their great success shows that it is not impossible to construct the three interdependent social systems—political, economic, and moral-cultural—that constitute the free society, in which free persons and free communities can flourish, and to do so within a relatively short time. This success gives heart to all who must achieve something similar, even if even more difficult.

Such a task, moreover, is never fully done, once and for all, but must often be recapitulated. For later generations need to rediscover the reasons why the free society is constructed as it is, and why it demands so many sacrifices and so much unrelenting effort. The price of the free society is unceasing reformation.

The free society is moral, or not at all. That is why it is so precarious. Any one generation, deciding that it is not worth the cost, can throw it over.

But the moral situation of the formerly communist countries is far more desperate than the situation of Germany in 1945. For the moral destruction that communism wrought in Russia during seventy-two years had time to plow far deeper into the primordial soil of the human spirit, and to be far more destructive of traditional institutions, practices, and associations. The damage to human capital was incalculable.

When my plane landed in St. Petersburg on September 10, 1991 (I had bought my ticket for Leningrad but when I landed it was St. Petersburg), the white, red, and blue flag of Russia was flying over the city for the first time in decades, in place of the red flag of communism. People in St. Petersburg were still exhilarated by their own heroism in standing for hours outside the Winter Palace in defense of the new constitution, surrounded by tanks and party photographers snapping their pictures for future prosecution. "Now we feel," a philosopher at the university told me in his apartment that night, "like normal people. We stood for our liberty just as Americans once did. We did it! You can't imagine how it felt, in front of the Winter Palace."

Later, in a more sober mood he told me, poking his finger into my chest, "Next time they try an experiment like socialism, they should try it out on animals first. Humans it hurts too much!"

He was brave and hopeful that night. I often wonder what his thoughts are now.

This much we know. Even under the best of conditions, it

is extremely difficult to construct a free society that works, that endures, that is self-correcting. The silent artillery that communism leveled at the human spirit and at every internal nerve of human capital for more than seventy years had its effect. The transition from communism to a free society is consequently a severely demanding moral task. It requires a transition from a monistic system to a threefold system, that is, to three relatively independent yet interdependent systems. It is a transition to a society free from torture, assassination, extortion, and tyranny in its political system; nourishing orderly and creative enterprise and liberating the poor from poverty in its economic system; and through its cultural system rewarding the habits that make a free economy and a free polity both possible and worthwhile.

How that transition goes is perhaps the greatest drama of our time. Everything depends on the use that humans make of the liberty with which each is endowed, while there is still time to affect the outcome. We are the *subjects* of this drama, not the *objects.*

Thomas Jefferson, no orthodox believer, put it this way: "The God who gave us life gave us liberty at the same time." It is no hindrance to our purposes to understand that liberty is the Creator's jewel, favored by Providence. Theism is no hindrance to personal dignity. On the contrary, it is its source.

In sum, the twin themes of this essay are not so disparate as at first glance they may appear. By its simultaneous hostility both to the human soul and to personal economic initiative, communism testified to their connection.

7

The End of Communist Economics

Andrzej Brzeski

Ideas have consequences.
—Richard Weaver

RATHER THAN SEARCHING for an answer to the question Why communist[1] economies collapsed? one should ask how they happened to survive as long as they in fact did. The economic system of the Soviet Union, later imposed also on Central and Eastern Europe, was fatally flawed from the very beginning. Irreparable despite many attempts, it was sustained by political structures and practices of the Marxist-Leninist party states. These states themselves could not last primarily, if not

I am indebted to Professor Alexander J. Groth for his comments and helpful suggestions.
    1. *Communism* and *communist* are used throughout to describe the realities of the Soviet bloc rather than the end-of-the-line utopia of Marx. The connection of the two is straightforward; the former (realities of the Soviet bloc) were meant to bring about the latter (Marx's utopia). For brevity's sake, the differences between countries are overlooked. The discussion deals with an ideal type.

only, because of faulty economics. It was literally a vicious circle. The story of the political decomposition and eventual downfall of communism is told elsewhere in this volume. This essay deals with matters of economics, but of course crossovers cannot be avoided.

Unlike capitalism (and earlier economic systems), which evolved gradually through adaptation to changing conditions, communism was a product of deliberate design. Its economic master plan had sprung ready-made from the heads of Marx and Engels. The basic idea, as expressed by Engels even before the publication of the *Manifesto*, was exceedingly simple, indeed naive:

> In communist society it will be easy to be informed about both production and consumption. Since we know how much, on the average, a person needs ... it is a trifling matter to regulate production according to needs.

Just as simple, Engels asserted, would also be the means:

> through society's taking out of the hands of private capitalists the use of all the productive forces and means of communication as well as the exchange and distribution of products and managing them according to a plan. . . . Society will produce enough products to be able so to arrange distribution that the needs of all its members will be satisfied.[2]

Ideas including the bad ones do have consequences. Adding to the key postulate of central planning of a state-owned economy—advocated in the quoted passage—some wrongheaded theory from *Das Kapital* yielded a prescription for economic

---

2. Frederick Engels in 1845 and 1847 in *Marx, Engels, Lenin on Communist Society* (Moscow: Progress Publications, 1978), pp. 10, 18.

trouble. Apparently, no one sufficiently persuasive was around to forewarn Lenin and Stalin, and those who might have tried were most likely dispatched to the Gulag.

Alexander Pushkin once wrote:

> Those who plan impossible revolutions in Russia are either youngsters who don't know . . . [the] people or positively heartless men who set little value on their own skins and less still on those of others.

His words came true. The early slogan "communism equals electrification plus Soviet power" should have been replaced by the less inspiring but more fitting "communism equals cerebration plus opportunity for the ruthless to act on their misconceptions." In building their new system, the communist social engineers rejected fact and sound theory in pursuit of a chimera.

Already twenty-three centuries ago, Aristotle saw the benefits of private ownership. "Property should be as a general rule private," he wrote, "for when everyone has a distinct interest, men . . . will make progress, because everyone will be attending to his own business." Adam Smith elaborated the same theme, in depth and rich detail, showing how self-interest, in a competitive private market, becomes a beneficial force and a source of progress. The emphasis on the importance of private ownership has been further strengthened by the Austrian school, in particular by Ludwig von Mises and Friedrich A. Hayek, and more recently by the so-called new institutional economics and its subdiscipline of property rights analysis, which explains how the advantages of private ownership can continue under the contemporary forms of corporate organization.

A "SUPERIOR" PLAN

Hayek's famous article on "The Use of Knowledge in Society" in particular shows why the market—which is the most effective, probably the only mechanism for generating and processing the information needed for allocation of resources in a complex economy—necessarily requires private ownership. But then, following Marx's idiosyncratic aversion, the communist social engineers rejected the market in favor of a supposedly superior plan. They also correspondingly dispensed with market-determined scarcity prices and adopted instead administrative pricing vaguely related to the discredited Marxian theory of value. The resultant muddle was complete. It combined a lackadaisical management of state-owned firms with irrelevant, frequently perverse information. With a considerable degree of managerial discretion due to incomplete and fuzzy plans, there was plenty of room for bad decisions. The hardships of daily life were the outcome for everyone to see.

Less obvious was the baneful effect of Marxian theory on the long-term economic prospects—capital accumulation. Arbitrary allocation of funds, concentrating the investment on the staples of communist-style industrialization—steel, heavy machinery, and basic chemicals—neglected not only consumer needs but also the industries of the future. The obsession with the role of heavy industry in economic progress (derived from a passage on the proportions of growth in *Das Kapital*) led to a lopsided production structure forever postponing the benefits of investment. Critics who characterized this pattern of industrialization as an input-input economy were proved right. The decades of sacrifice did not pay off. They created a badly inefficient economy, locked out from full participation in world trade, unable to satisfy the ordinary needs of the populace or to maintain adequate rates of growth. In one writer's apt phrase, the Communists had succeeded in creating "an impressive XIX century infrastructure some seventy-five years too late."

Comparisons of national product or income of different countries over a long haul are treacherous. This is especially so in the case of communist countries, where the reliability and economic relevance of statistics are highly problematic. Nonetheless, the available estimates suggest that, by the end of the 1980s, the relative position of the Soviet bloc countries vis-à-vis their "reference group"—the West—had actually deteriorated since 1929.

Hundreds of books and thousands of articles chronicled communist economic developments, but in most of them the role of Marxist doctrine in shaping institutions and policies was given slight notice. Instead, expediency and bureaucratic self-interest were usually stressed. This is understandable; public choice theory fully applies to the communist case. Once the party-state apparat is in place, managing things, it resists changes threatening its prerogatives and rewards. Bureaucratic infighting among opposing interests (for instance, regional versus sectoral or light versus heavy industry) spills into the political arena and, in effect, decisively influences organization and policies. This was clearly demonstrated during Khrushchev's tenure. Yet underneath, and prior to all the rent seeking, were the determinants of the existing structures and their special interests. The *causa causans* could be found in the now rarely read books of the "classics" of Marxism-Leninism.

Replacing private property rights with state ownership gave rise to a huge class of functionaries committed to preserving and, when opportune, extending their specific domains. Although the communist economic system had other characteristic aspects, the abolition of private property was its most important, indeed *defining* feature. Coupled with its logical complement, central planning, it also was the root cause of the economic dysfunctionality afflicting communist countries. The inefficiency of state-owned industries was notorious and continued unabated despite a great many attempts to repair the system. Production was generally lacking in quality and out of touch with consumer demand. Inventories of goods no one wanted kept piling up, whereas there were acute shortages of just about everything people wanted to buy. Moreover costs were rising, with materials and labor squandered; investment projects dragged on interminably, sometimes abandoned halfway and often underutilized on completion. The catalog of economic delinquencies could be infinitely expanded; central planning was visibly failing to allocate resources in a satisfactory manner.

THE SOVIET MILITARY-INDUSTRIAL COMPLEX

Naturally, the communist leaders' priorities outweighed all other needs. Forced draft industrialization, and its banner projects—Dnieprostroi, Nowa Huta, and the like—were pushed at breakneck pace regardless of cost, as were all projects directly related to the military. Everything else was treated as a buffer sector, subject to reductions and general neglect. Perpetuating low consumption standards and technological disparities, communist planners, above all the Soviet ones, seemed to have succeeded mainly in one respect: building up an enormous war machine. According to an apt characterization by Abraham Becker, the United States *had* an industrial-military complex, but the Soviet Union *was* such a complex. On top of the heavy burden of investment (amounting possibly to 40 percent of the national product), military expenditures were among the highest in the world in relative terms. No wonder the consumers felt squeezed. The party-state, which, following the prescription of the "classics" of Marxism-Leninism, had usurped the right to control all the means of production, was totally blocking off their influence on allocation of resources. The state, which owned everything, was putting things to its own uses. Inevitably, this kind of an economic system was connected with a high degree of political oppression.

Still, for decades, communist leaders boasted of success. The outside reaction to their schemes was mostly that of puzzlement, but quite often, apart from the fundamental criticism by some academics, notably the already mentioned Mises and Hayek, the assessment was favorable and became a source of reassurance. In the beginning, it was the starry-eyed enthusiasm of the left-leaning intelligentsia that set the tone. The much-quoted American journalist Lincoln Steffens provides an emblematic example: "I have been over to the future, and it works," he declared, returning from Russia in 1919. This was during the period of war communism, which, through strictest regimentation, brought the country to catastrophic conditions, forcing Lenin to a tactical retreat into the quasi-capitalism of the New Economic Policy (NEP).

No sooner did Stalin reverse the policies of the NEP, by introducing the institutions and practices that with only minor modifications were to survive for over half a century, than the chorus of approval resumed, on a still higher note. The learned Webbs' praise of the "new civilization" was a case in point. They wrote:

> The socialist economy has certain natural advantages . . . it is not limited by the demand of profit, nor hampered by private property rights. . . . In addition, a planned economy can

secure the most productive distribution of credit. It can build
the biggest and best equipped enterprises. It can use machinery up to the operating point of the law of diminishing returns.
. . . Also a planned economy permits, for the first time, a
scientific development of natural resources.[3]

Similarly enthusiastic about the new social and economic
order was, in his *Rationalization of Russia*, another notable,
George Bernard Shaw. There were a great many others as well,
including journalists and sober men of affairs, impressed by
the gigantic projects of the five-year plans. Hopes for doing
business with the communist giant were high, especially
among Americans and Germans plagued at the time by the
Great Depression. The story is all too familiar.

In the 1950s and 1960s, the growth of the communist
countries was judged impressive enough by many outsiders to
offset the seemingly clear failings of their economic performance. As Peter Wiles pithily put it: "they eye our efficiency,
we eye their growth." Full, even overfull, employment combined with high rates of investment to produce a pace of
growth that, at the time, captured the imagination of many in
the West. The availability of health services and education, as
well as egalitarian tenets, was deemed a sufficient reason for
overlooking the oppressive nature of communism and its bla-
tant economic defects. According to British Labour's Richard
Crossman, the Soviet Communists were merely engaged in
building an "ordinary society" by "horrible means." (At least
he abhorred the means.)

3. Sidney and Beatrice Webb, *Soviet Communism: A New Civilization?*
(New York: Scribner, 1936), p. 648.

SOVIET "SUCCESS"

Such distaste was largely absent in the proliferating academic works in which the Soviet way was described as a successful mobilization regime, perhaps the only way to impose modernity, and a measure of affluence, on those who have fallen behind. Thus, in John H. Kautsky's reassuring view,

> the Russian Revolution [fits] into the broad historical pattern
> of the nationalist revolutions in underdeveloped countries.[4]

In the literature on "mobilization," Romania's Ceauçescu was held out as an example, in contrast to less effectual leaders. According to Kenneth Jowitt, under Ceauçescu's leadership:

> It may well be that given its goal of mobilization—breaking
> through and industrialization—the directive and coercive
> posture of the Romanian elite was appropriate to the Roma-
> nian context.[5]

China, which has established itself as a new paradigm of communism, was greatly admired (e.g., Joan Robinson in *Economic Management in China*) for its sundry surreal campaigns that were believed to speed a transition from feudalism to utopia.

There was, of course, a growing specialized literature on the functioning of communist economies in which the defects and malfunctioning of the system were duly noted and ana-

4. John H. Kautsky, *Communism and the Politics of Development: Persistent Myths and Changing Behavior* (New York: Wiley & Sons, 1968), p. 82.

5. Kenneth Jowitt, *Revolutionary Breakthroughs and National Development: The Case of Romania 1944–1965* (Berkeley: University of California Press, 1971), p. 124.

lyzcd. Moreover, with the eruption of hostility to communism in East Germany, Poland, Hungary, and Czechoslovakia during the mid-1950s, the tenor of Western opinion began to change. The evermore striking defects of communist planning and management made it obvious that everything was not well in the countries ruled by Communists. An interminable discussion took place, in which the putative ways to streamline and improve communism were dissected; even a cursory account cannot be attempted here. Simplifying the story however, its proverbial "bottom line" was that, even in the more critical analysis, the details obscured the gist.

Apart from some perceptive discussions of agriculture, the absence of private property was hardly ever considered decisive. Consequently, blueprints of so-called market socialism were being dusted off and tentatively offered as a possible improvement. But the *res sacra* of communism, the socialized means of production—in practical terms, state ownership—was rarely mentioned as the reason for unsatisfactory performance. In a far-sighted article Warren G. Nutter described such notions thirty years ago as "Markets without Property Rights: A Grand Illusion." His doubts about communism's ability to reform itself were obviously not shared by practical men; a steady stream of corporate leaders hoping to do business with Soviet and other Communists testifies to this. Suffice to mention in this connection the likes of Pepsi Cola's Donald Kendall, Armco's John Giffen, and, of course, the legendary Armand Hammer or, more important yet, the bankers and finance ministers eagerly proffering tens of billions of dollars in loans to communist governments. Ironically, it was the extensive state ownership in particular that accounted for the lenders' confidence. How could one go wrong lending to regimes that owned *everything*? As history tells us, one certainly could, to the tune of a hundred billion dollars if not more.

With the increasing complexity of the industrializing economies, their failings were becoming evermore evident. Engels's simpleminded fantasies about the advantages of central planning in a state-owned economy notwithstanding, it was becoming widely recognized that a central authority (even one equipped with computers rather than the still dominant abaci and slide rules) was incapable of preparing a consistent, not to mention efficient, plan. Needless to say, the planners never came close to full control of the economy. They had always formulated many output (and input) targets in aggregates (rubles, zlotys, etc.) rather than natural units. The difficulty with that, however, was twofold. First, the aggregates, expressed in value terms, were economically meaningless because of arbitrary pricing. Second, the managers of state-owned firms could not be induced to make the "right" choices. In fact, they were not even in the position to know what a right choice would be. Naturally, they suited their own preferences, which seldom coincided with the interest of the public. Without the guidance of a price system and the restraint of competition, the results quite often offended common sense. Mises and Hayek had their revenge. Planning in reality boiled down to ad hoc interventions, thus illustrating on a grand scale Ambrose Bierce's aphorism that to plan is "to bother about the best method of accomplishing an accidental result."

FALLING SHORT EVERYWHERE

A Soviet cartoon, in which a factory's production consisted of an enormous single nail because the bonus was tied to the total weight of output, epitomized a real problem of communist economics. A number of attempts were undertaken in all parts of the communist bloc in the 1960s and 1970s to improve performance. However, fixing the system without abandoning its most distinctive property and planning principles fell short of expectations everywhere, even in the case of the once popular new economic mechanism in Hungary and the East German new economic system.

Foreign trade, normally an essential part of the machinery of economic progress in capitalist economies, also suffered at the hands of the ruling Marxist-Leninists. Trading mostly bilaterally among themselves—in effect, bartering—Soviet bloc countries were unable to reap the benefits of comparative advantage. The coordinating agency for intrabloc trade and cooperation—the COMECON—was one more entirely superfluous layer of the planning bureaucracy. Because of distorted national price systems and arbitrary multiple exchange rates, nobody could calculate the net effects of trade; it was not unusual for both sides of a deal to consider themselves exploited. As the communist economies expanded, their imports and exports went up too. Yet, by comparison with the rest of the world, the commercial expansion was relatively modest. The ratios of trade to total output figures were lower than elsewhere. Moreover, by various indications, the trade was also less advantageous. Trade with the West seemed, and probably was, more promising, but it was circumscribed by currency inconvertibility and other political, institutional, and procedural peculiarities of the centrally planned economies. In this respect, there were changes for the better in some countries during the 1970s, but by then it was too late to make a real difference.

By the 1970s, some new difficulties arose in addition to the usual old ones. The economic engine of communism was running out of steam. Reserves of un- and underemployed rural labor, which had been crucial earlier in the forced industrialization drive, were well-nigh exhausted. At the same time, further increases of investment at the expense of consumption became technically difficult and, because of the weakening political control over the population, seemed politically risky. The extensive type of growth—fueled by ever-increasing factor inputs—was reaching its limits.

Viewed from another perspective, it was a problem of savings. The large capital outlays required by the earlier communist industrialization programs were financed, especially in the Soviet Union, by forced savings of the peasantry. Originally, quite apart from the doctrinal bias, this was what the collectivization campaign was about; to feed industrial workers, grain and meat were taken away at confiscatory prices. The peasants starved. Later, and with greatly increased need for agricultural products, this source of forced savings began to dry up. The peasantry, drastically reduced in numbers, had to be motivated by incentives to increase supplies. Accordingly, the acquisition prices of farm produce were constantly raised and the obligatory delivery quotas lowered. Moreover, to compensate for the diminished labor input, agricultural capital investment had to be considerably increased. Thus, instead of serving, in accord with Stalin's recipe, as the source of primitive communist accumulation, agriculture greedily absorbed funds generated elsewhere. Details differed by country, but the drying up of the peasantry's forced savings was a feature of the economic retardation, especially in the Soviet Union and Poland.

With the vaunted communist tempo slowing, Soviet boasts about catching up with (and overtaking) the United States became demonstrably hollow. Other countries of the bloc found themselves in an analogous situation; they were obviously making no progress in their own catching up with the West. Discussion about the "barriers to growth" testified to the awareness of the problem in the countries of the Soviet bloc. Looking for ways to break through the limitations, communist leaders put their hopes in intensive growth attributable to technical (and organizational) progress. This somewhat vaguely defined source of growth had accounted for a large part—one-half to three-quarters—of production gains under capitalism. In the communist context of state ownership and planning, however, it was distressingly smaller. In this respect too, the communist system was a disappointment.

WESTERN BILLIONS

As in the 1930s, when imports of equipment had provided a vital ingredient of Stalin's industrialization, this time too the solution was temporarily sought in the capitalist West. Buoyed by détente, the West obliged, providing tens of billions of dollars in subsidized loans, export licenses, and other amenities. Communist regimes expected to modernize their economies this way, but in mounting disorganization, the resources acquired from the West were rarely productively used. Billions of dollars' worth of imported equipment were going to waste, often still crated. Additional billions of foreign credit were dissipated on politically motivated consumption boosts. Some party leaders—Brezhnev, Gierek, and Kadar—gained popularity by financing consumption with Western largesse. They might have believed that, by placating the public, they were gaining time to complete the big turnaround to "intensification of growth." Gierek's upbeat slogan appealing to national pride, "The Poles can do it" (*Polak potrafi*) epitomized such optimism. Yet, again retrospectively, communist hopes were bound to be disappointed; the awakened appetites of long-deprived people could not be satisfied that easily. Stalin knew that much when he tried—successfully—to shield his subjects from the demonstration effect of unattainable living standards. Brezhnev and Gierek did not.

From the point of view of the consumer, the decades-long communist experiment was calamitous. Not only were shortages and a poor quality of goods of every description endemic, but housing conditions were critical. Moreover, many services that ordinarily enhance living standards were altogether lacking. Cleaning and laundry establishments were simply nonexistent. In travel amenities and telephone availability, the Soviet Union and some of the bloc countries ranked among the least developed in the world. In 1981, illustrating this aspect of communist backwardness, there were more hotel and motel establishments in Sacramento, California, than in all of the Soviet Union open to foreign visitors. Retail and restaurant industries were, even by official figures, grotesquely underdeveloped in relation to the outside world. Life under communism was difficult indeed.

Perforce, the communist economic system was highly politicized. A creation of Marxist-Leninist party leaders, planned and managed by appointed party apparatchiks, it was in every respect a truly *political economy*. In the last phase of its unraveling during the 1980s, in particular the late 1980s, political and economic developments were interwoven so closely that their separate treatment would be impossible. The vicious circle worked itself out fully. Bad economics and futile attempts at reform undermined the party-state, which in turn contributed to further deterioration of the economy, weakening the party-state even further. With the politboros desperately trying to mend their ways by curtailing terror (to gain legitimacy), little was needed to trigger the terminal crisis.

At the beginning of the 1980s, a new external source of pressure confronted the Soviet Union, with ultimate consequences for all the other bloc countries as well. Under the leadership of President Ronald Reagan, the United States was stepping up its military preparedness in conventional and nuclear forces, and it was doing so with ever-increasing emphasis on sophisticated technologies. Reagan's antimissile defense program symbolized the larger trend that put a great strain on Soviet resources. The Kremlin was faced with an unpalatable choice: to match the new U.S. initiatives by significantly increasing military expenditure or to accede to U.S. superiority. The prospect of increasing military budgets was in conflict with all hopes for improving living conditions for the long-suffering Soviet consumers. A drastic "tightening of the screws" would have required a return to Stalin-like domestic repression, which most likely would provoke popular unrest. Clearly, such considerations weighed heavily on Mikhail Gorbachev and his politburo associates. Be that as it may, a series of interrelated events throughout the Soviet bloc set the stage, with the Polish Solidarity movement posing an unanswerable challenge and Gorbachev signaling a retreat.

ECONOMIC DIFFICULTIES, POLITICAL PARALYSIS

At all times during the prolonged denouement the economic situation was deteriorating, especially in Gorbachev's Soviet Union and in martial law–ruled Poland. Gorbachev himself was optimistic. With typical verbosity he insisted that his

> concept of economic reform . . . is of an all-embracing, comprehensive character . . . [and] provides for fundamental changes in every area, including the transfer of enterprises to complete cost accounting, a radical transformation of the economy, fundamental changes in planning, a reform of the

price formation system and of the financial and crediting mechanism, and the restructuring of foreign economic ties. It also provides for the creation of new organizational structures of management, for the all-round development of the democratic foundation of management, and for the broad introduction to the self-management principles.[6]

Unluckily for him, however, the realities were refractory. In the course of perestroika, endless reorganizations aiming at devolution of decision making brought chaos instead. By commission and omission, mostly the latter, firms were quasi-privatized by local *nomenklatura*. They engaged in barter and defied all central direction. Because of a weakening of wage controls and financial discipline, inflationary pressures were building up dangerously. A political paralysis on all levels—from the politburo to factory committees—accentuated the economic difficulties. As constructed, the system could not function at all without a strong center. The situation in other communist bloc countries differed in specifics, but all were strongly affected by the turmoil and confusion in Moscow and also approaching a critical point.

By repudiating the 1968 Brezhnev Doctrine in favor of the so-called 1988 Sinatra Doctrine (everyone should do things in their own way), Gorbachev all but induced an accelerated disintegration of the communist system throughout the Soviet bloc. Gorbachev's new stand put the local leaders in an untenable position. They were pressured at home but could no longer count on the threat of Soviet intervention. As soon as conditions began to approach free choice, the people did in 1989 what they would have most likely done in 1950, 1960,

---

6. Mikhail Gorbachev, *Perestroika: New Thinking for Our Country and the World* (New York: Harper & Row, 1987), p. 84.

1970, or 1980 if they could have—they abandoned communism.

Polish Communists, pressed by a mass movement inspired by John Paul II and led by Solidarity, were the first to draw the inescapable conclusion: the experiment was over. Having half-heartedly agreed to an orderly exit early in 1989, they proceeded to lose a parliamentary election in June of that year, and were out of power by September, when the Mazowiecki government was installed by a freely elected parliament. Only two months later, even *before* the symbolic wall was torn down in Berlin, the Polish cabinet adopted a comprehensive program of dismantling communism and replacing it with ordinary capitalist institutions. The rest is history, with other bloc countries, including the several successor states of the Soviet Union, following the lead, each after its own fashion.

The subsequent path has not been easy. The legacies of communism have posed obstacles, in some cases perhaps for decades to come. Painful economic and social adjustments, perhaps political instability, might lie ahead, especially where the communist system was most deeply entrenched: Russia, Ukraine, and other post-Soviet republics. Nonetheless, whatever the circumstances, another attempt at making communist economics work appears unlikely.

Surveying the remains of the old regime in the former Soviet Union and the countries of Central and Eastern Europe is instructive. The human cost of terror and oppression is naturally a crime in itself; it must not be forgotten. In more material terms, there are other lessons to remember. The commitment to state ownership instead of private ownership and to central planning instead of the market mechanism inflicted permanent injury on the communist economies.

On one hand, the incentives to work hard, to save, and to invest were undermined. The hope and opportunity of making a profit were replaced by a relatively stagnant wage and salary system. The rewards were generally unrelated to productivity, creativity, or thrift. People were rewarded for "putting in the time." The communist ideological commitment to full employment shielded even the most lazy and incompetent from a powerful incentive known to capitalism: loss of a job. To be sure, there were bonuses and "public recognition" for the members of the shock brigades—the Soviet Stakhanovites. But these were marginal incentives. Besides, the bonuses, awarded according to criteria set by central planners, could actually compound the distortions of the communist economies, encouraging production of shoddy and unwanted goods or the building of obsolete industrial plants.

THE ROLE OF HUMAN CAPITAL

For many people in all societies, accumulating wealth to pass on to one's children and grandchildren is a most important motivating force—a this-world realization of one's immortality. This has always constituted an incentive for work and achievement. Clearly, the pursuit of wealth would frequently and quite naturally involve the "means of production and distribution" and various other forms of assets proscribed to private individuals by the Marxists. A society deprived of such opportunities to amass wealth is also a society in which the mainsprings of material progress—technical and economic—are blocked. The acquisition of the all-important human capital—knowledge, skills, and attitudes supportive of entrepreneurship—is all but eliminated, leading to impoverishment not only in the present but also in the future. It is, no doubt, the lack of human capital that accounts for the most crippling obstacles to postcommunist transition in today's

Russia and some other post-Soviet countries. Medals and party praise cannot make up for that.

On the planning end of the Marxist formula, the question of what would be produced and consumed within the economy was taken out of the hands of the public (normally voting, as it were, with their money) and put into the hands of party-state bureaucrats. Enormous frustrations and deprivations were inevitable under these arrangements, especially since the part of total output devoted to consumption, reduced by over-blown capital investment and military expenditures, was piti-fully small.

Given these "permanent problems" of communism, and looking back at its decades-long record, it seems to be the case that Stalinism, far from being an aberration in the system, was its most logical and functional component. Only the sustained use of force, credible terror, and an artificially maintained sense of isolation of the society from the international envi-ronment could keep the communist system from collapsing. For Stalin and his imitators, the cold war and perpetual prepa-rations for war had distinctive domestic advantages. Indeed, Stalin was able to maintain the communist regime from the 1920s into the 1950s, extending its reach over another hundred million Central and Eastern Europeans, and even give it super-power status despite low, even falling living standards for the people of the Soviet Union. The real political difficulties began with the successive Soviet and East European reformers, cul-minating in Gorbachev, because, in addition to détente, they sought to accomplish the impossible: make a fundamentally unnatural and inefficient economic system rest on popular consent.

In conclusion, Alec Nove's question "Was Stalin Necessary?" should probably be answered in the affirmative by those trying to understand how communist economies survived until the last decade of our millennium. It took a Stalin and his lingering influence to make possible the implementation, over several decades, of the very bad ideas of Marxism-Leninism.

8

Why the Cold War?

Brian Crozier

WHY INDEED was there a cold war? Most wars are military and their causes are many. The cold war, unlike conventional military wars, was not initially a clash between rival national armies; it was sparked by secret political maneuvers, the aims of which were not immediately understood because of the secrecy that enveloped them. Although the term *cold war* suggests that it was nonmilitary, in fact it included a number of military engagements, and its "cold" character applied only to the absence of such engagements between the two superpowers—the Soviet Union and the United States—or between their respective alliances: the Warsaw Pact and NATO.

What, exactly, was the cold war? It was certainly more complex than the public at large realized. There was a "secret espionage war," waged in effect by the secret services of the opposing sides: the Soviet KGB and GRU (military intelligence) on the enemy side, with the corresponding secret services of all the satellites (Czechoslovakia, Hungary, etc., and, later, Cuba); countered by the Western agencies, especially the American Central Intelligence Agency (CIA) and the British SIS (Secret Intelligence Service, better known as MI-6). There was also a semisecret subversive propaganda war, countered on a smaller scale by the Western powers. There was a military "war" of nerves, the main feature of which was a nuclear confrontation and, not least, a war of peripheral colonization by the Soviet Union, starting in the 1960s with the satellization of Cuba and intensified in the 1970s and 1980s. Finally, there was a real war of military invasion, waged by the Soviet Union against Afghanistan.

Various Western thinkers and analysts have fastened on different events as marking the start of the cold war. An interesting example was James Burnham, whom I regard as my mentor in the skills and methods of political thinking. In one of his early works, *The Struggle for the World* (1947), he gave a precise date for the start of what he called the Third World War: April 1947, when a communist-led mutiny broke out in the Greek navy in the Egyptian harbor of Alexandria.

True, this apparently unimportant event has to be seen in the context of communist-led guerrilla attacks on other resistance groups in Greece fighting the German-Italian occupation of their country. But in the light of later revelations, I would give the cold war an earlier starting date: May 1943. On the fifteenth of that month, to be precise, Moscow announced the dissolution of the communist Third International, better known as the Comintern. Stalin declared that this decision "exposed the lie of the Hitlerites to the effect that Moscow allegedly intends to intervene in the life of other countries and to Bolshevise them. . . . It exposes the calumny . . . that Communist parties in various countries are allegedly acting not in the interests of their people but on orders from outside."

The full significance of this apparently conciliatory move did not emerge until nearly thirty years later. At the time, it was seen as Stalin's mollifying response to complaints from the Soviet Union's Western allies about continuing Soviet-backed subversion against Western political systems. In 1974, however, it emerged from the testimonies of various Soviet defectors that the "dissolution" of the Comintern was one of the biggest and most effective of Soviet deceptions. On paper, the Comintern had ceased to exist; in reality, its functions had simply been transferred to the International Department of the ruling Communist Party of the Soviet Union (CPSU)—actually styled at that time the "All Union Communist Party (Bolshevik)."

These random examples illustrate the world range of the Soviet subversive apparatus. As it happened, the postwar governments of the West were led by relatively inexperienced politicians: the United States by Harry Truman, the United Kingdom by Clement Attlee. In the crucial transitional period from war to peace, it is now known that the dying president F. D. Roosevelt's special envoy to Stalin, Harry Hopkins, had been recruited by the Soviet secret service as an agent of influence, who skillfully disinformed the president on the Soviet leader's intentions.

Astonishing as it now seems, Britain's wartime leader, Prime Minister Winston Churchill, as well as Roosevelt, had been taken in by Stalin, as demonstrated by his speech in the House of Commons on his return from the Yalta Conference in February 1945:

> The impression I brought back from the Crimea, and from all my other contacts, is that Marshal Stalin and the Soviet leaders wish to live in honorable friendship and equality with the Western democracies. I feel also that their word is their bond.

> I know of no government which stands to its obligations, even
> in its own despite, more solidly than the Russian Soviet gov-
> ernment. I decline absolutely to embark here on a discussion
> about Russian good faith.[1]

At war's end, the widely accepted view of Josef Stalin's
foreign policy was that, unlike Leon Trotsky, he had abandoned the concept of world revolution. He was seen as a leader
whose limited ambition was to build "socialism" in his own
country. In February 1946, Stalin himself shattered the non-
communist world when he publicly declared that the doctrine
of world revolution was still valid.

More than thirty of the world's communist parties had
been set up during the lifetime of Vladimir Lenin, the em-
balmed founder and leader of the international communist
machine who died in January 1924. Some fifty more were set
up after his death, beyond the death of his successor, Stalin, in
1953, and indeed into the 1960s. All of them, to a greater or
lesser degree, were subsidized and ultimately controlled by
Moscow, despite occasional assertions of independence before
being brought to heel by threats or repression from the CPSU's
Comintern (short for Third International) or its successor, the
International Department. To emphasize this crucially important reality, one of the ultimate Russian apparatchiks, Boris
Ponomarev, who had been a member of the Executive Committee of the Comintern under Stalin, was appointed head of
the International Department, under the overall guidance of
Mikhail Suslov, the Kremlin's ideological leader.

Stalin wasted little time after the defeat of nazi Germany
and its Japanese ally before ordering the revitalizing and ex-

---

1. Winston Churchill, *The Second World War* (London: Cassell, 1954),
vol. 12, chap. 4, "Yalta Finale."

pansion of the world's communist parties, in 1946, to be precise. That year saw the launching of parties in East Germany (Sozialistische Einheitspartei Deutschlands) and Laos (Pasachon Lao). Nigeria's Socialist Workers' and Farmers' Party (SWAFF) was started even earlier, in 1943.[2]

In the immediate aftermath of World War II, there was understandably a wave of public euphoria in the West about Russia and its leader. Long forgotten, or forgiven, was the Stalin-Hitler pact of August 23, 1939; the Soviet Union had been "our glorious ally." This view was not necessarily shared in Western official circles; but even there, in both the United States and Britain, it would emerge later that Stalin's NKVD had placed pro-Soviet spies or agents of influence, including Alger Hiss in the United States and Kim Philby in Britain.

Between 1946 and 1948, threatening crises arose in Greece, Turkey, Iran, Czechoslovakia, and Germany (with special emphasis on Berlin). During this critical period two headline-catching expressions joined the international vocabulary. One was the theme of this chapter; it was in 1947 that the American financier and presidential adviser Bernard Baruch first used the term *cold war.*

Another contribution to the international vocabulary came from Winston Churchill, at Fulton, Missouri, in March 1946, when Churchill, in a resounding speech, used the term *Iron Curtain.* Ironically, this term—since then permanently associated with Churchill—had actually been coined by Goebbels, Hitler's propaganda chief. The term did, however, symbolically fit the division between East and West created by Stalin after Hitler's defeat.

Those who understood the reality of communism as a world threat included two diplomatic officials—unknown to

2. *Yearbook on Communist Affairs* (Stanford: Hoover Institution, 1966).

the public at that time—each of whom played an important role in responding to what amounted to Stalin's declaration of the cold war on the West. The American one was George F. Kennan, at that time chargé d'affaires in Moscow; the British one was Christopher Mayhew, parliamentary undersecretary of state for foreign affairs in Britain's postwar Labour government of Clement Attlee.

In both cases, the initial blow for freedom was struck in secret. Kennan's took the form of a dispatch to the State Department (the "Long Telegram"), analyzing the Soviet government's "neurotic" view of the outside world exacerbated by two invasions in thirty years and a tyrannical regime's near-paranoid obsession with political insecurity. Marxism, he reasoned, was seen by the Soviets as justifying hostility toward the West. He advocated a policy of "containment" of Soviet expansionism.

On March 12, 1947, President Truman announced a far-reaching program of economic aid to Greece and Turkey, which became known as the "Truman Doctrine" and incorporated the arguments of Kennan including the concept of "containment." The Truman Doctrine was also a response to a dispatch from the British government to the effect that British aid to Greece would have to end in six weeks, despite the deteriorating military situation. Truman's declaration made it clear, however, that U.S. support would not be limited to Greece and Turkey.

A slightly sanitized version of Kennan's dispatch appeared in the July 1947 issue of the quarterly *Foreign Affairs*, which created an international sensation. In line with the diplomatic rule of anonymity, Kennan's name did not appear; the article was signed X. It went on to advocate a "long-term, patient but firm and vigilant policy of containment of Russian expansive tendencies . . . with unalterable counter-force at every point where they show signs of encroaching upon the interests of a peaceful and stable world."[3]

The Truman Doctrine was given an economic dimension by the then secretary of state, General George C. Marshall, in a vast program of assistance to the European countries to set them on the path of recovery from the devastation of World War II. As originally conceived, the Marshall Plan (as it became known) was an offer to all of the warring countries united against nazi Germany, including the Soviet Union. Stalin immediately rejected the offer and forbade the new Soviet satellites to accept U.S. aid.

In Great Britain, the junior minister Christopher Mayhew, mentioned earlier, drafted a secret paper issued in October 1946 entitled "The Strategic Aspects of British Foreign Policy," which provided an accurate diagnosis of the Soviet challenge. The document had been prepared for Britain's Chiefs of Staff and had been sent to them by Sir Orme Sargent, at that time the permanent undersecretary (in effect the chairman) of the Foreign Office.

The British foreign secretary was Ernest Bevin, who had been the leader of his country's largest trade union, the Transport and General Workers, a "rough diamond," undereducated but intelligent and of strong character. His number two was Hector McNeil, and Mayhew ranked as number three. At thirty-two, Mayhew was the youngest of the three, and his secret document was a shrewd and effective response to the challenge of Soviet subversive propaganda: a new division of

---

3. For a full coverage of this period in American history, see Brian Crozier, Drew Middleton, and Jeremy Murray-Brown, *This War Called Peace* (London: Sherwood, 1984), chap. 3, "Where the Buck Stopped" (unsigned but written by the late Drew Middleton, at that time a senior foreign correspondent of the *New York Times*). Henceforth, *This War*.

the Foreign Office, to be named the Information Research Department (IRD).

A modest, self-effacing man, Mayhew defined his diagnosis
in his 1987 autobiography, entitled *Time to Explain*:

> At this time, Stalin's worldwide campaign of subversion and
> propaganda was at its most effective. Orchestrated from Mos-
> cow, . . . scores of communist or communist-front organiza-
> tions maintained a relentless war against Western govern-
> ments and institutions. The Soviet Union was presented as
> the exact antithesis of the West, that is, as the true enemy of
> Fascism, the champion of colonial peoples against imperial-
> ism, the ally of all peace-loving peoples against imperialism,
> and the shining example of a workers' state in which capital-
> ism had been abolished and where the workers prospered and
> were free.
>
> To this flood of propaganda, the Western countries made
> no organised response at all.[4]

Mayhew's proposed remedy was an ideological counteroffensive against Stalinism. He briefed Bevin, who decided to
support him and who in turn briefed the prime minister,
Clement Attlee, who gave the go-ahead and indeed launched
the counteroffensive in a broadcast on the BBC's World Service.

Mayhew's concept—the IRD—went on to become the largest department of Britain's Foreign Office, with an annual budget reaching £1 million a year (depending on a variable exchange rate, on average, about $1.6 million). The guiding
principles of IRD were, in my view, admirable. They included
accuracy and objectivity. The aim was to counter Soviet sub-

---

4. Christopher Mayhew, *Time to Explain* (London, 1987), p. 106.

versive propaganda, a major aim of which was to spread offensive falsehoods. The tone was unemotional, the range worldwide. There were reports on Asian and Latin American as well as European affairs. There were even items about the communist penetration of Britain's trade unions (thus stretching the Foreign Office's approved range of duties into domestic politics). IRD's methods were interesting. The department built up a wide but carefully selected list of recipients for its publications, who could make whatever use they wished of the information or intelligence provided, on condition that they kept the sources to themselves. They included a considerable number of journalists, the author of this chapter among them. The IRD also ventured into financing a number of books, not least a series entitled Background Books, published by Bodley Head in London.

Ironically, since the IRD was launched by a Labour government, it was closed by a later one. In 1974, when the Conservative government of Edward Heath yielded to Harold Wilson's Labour Party in the midst of a devastating strike of coal miners, IRD suspended all of its reports on subversion in Britain. Three years later, with Labour still in power, the foreign secretary, David Owen, took the decision to close down the Information Research Department. The reason given was that the "private circulation list had become suspect."[5]

THE BERLIN CONFERENCE

The Truman administration addressed the problem of subversive propaganda in a strikingly different but highly effective manner, through the Central Intelligence Agency (CIA). Once

5. Brian Crozier, *Free Agent: The Unseen War, 1941–1991* (New York: HarperCollins, 1993), p. 120.

again, and for sound reasons, secrecy reigned. An international conference of Western "intellectuals"—which attracted an audience of fifteen thousand—was convened, symbolically in Berlin, on June 29, 1950. As it happened, the starting date was four days after communist North Korea had triggered the Korean War by invading South Korea: the first hot incident of the cold war. The participants included a considerable number of famous Western writers. One of them, Arthur Koestler, was the ex-communist author of the powerful political novel *Darkness at Noon*. His words included these:

> The theory and practice of the totalitarian state are the greatest challenge which man has been called upon to meet in the course of civilised history. . . . Indifference or neutrality in the face of such a challenge amounts to a betrayal of mankind and to the abdication of the free mind.[6]

The congress yielded two practical outcomes: a pamphlet entitled *The Freedom Manifesto* and, on a long-term basis, a new international organization called the Congress for Cultural Freedom.[7] The CCF, in turn, launched a wide range of magazines or reviews in different countries and languages, the most celebrated of which was the monthly *Encounter*, published in London and edited for many years by the American Melvin Lasky, who had long worked on an American anticommunist fortnightly, *New Leader*.

Arthur Koestler was only one of a number of founder-members of the CCF who had been members of communist parties.

6. Paul Lashmar and James Oliver, *Britain's Secret Propaganda War 1948–1977* (London, 1999).

7. The fullest description of the birth of the CCF and its subsequent life is by the Australian writer Peter Coleman, in *The Liberal Conspiracy: The Congress for Cultural Freedom and the Struggle for the Mind of Postwar Europe* (New York and London: Macmillan, 1989).

Others included the Germans Franz Borkenau and Ruth Fischer, and the Italian Ignazio Silone.

James Burnham, an ex-Trotskyist, was also involved. Well-known writers or academics included the American historian Arthur Schlesinger Jr., the British philosophers Bertrand Russell and A. J.Ayer as well as the historian Hugh Trevor-Roper and the Frenchmen André Gide and Denis de Rougemont.

For many years, the main financial supporter of the CCF was said to be the Ford Foundation, but in time the truth came out: the Ford Foundation, in the jargon of the time, was a "notional donor." The true one was of course the CIA. The ultimate organizer was the American Michael Josselson, whose employer (it was later revealed) was also the Central Intelligence Agency.

Apart from *Encounter* in Britain, the CCF also launched and supported a number of other magazines in different countries, including *Preuves* in France, *Der Monat* in Germany, *Tempo Presente* in Italy, *Quadrant* in Australia, *Quest* in India, *Cuadernos* in Argentina, and *Cadernos Brasileiros* in Brazil.

Nor were the British Foreign Office and the CIA alone in fighting the enemies of the West during the cold war. Two French secret organizations also played their part: the SDECE (Service de Documentation Extérieure et de Contre-espionnage—France's equivalent of the American CIA or Britain's MI-6), and the Cinquième Bureaux, charged with military countersubversion. Both the French organizations were initially charged with improving Franco-German relations (after three Franco-German wars: in 1870, 1914, and 1939). Both organized semisecret international gatherings, which broadened their spheres by inviting nationals of other European countries and later American and Latin American participants in conferences in defense of the West against Soviet subversion.[8] The CIA further broadened its range of activities by running an information service, initially styled *Forum*, largely devoted to cultural questions and distributed free of charge but later commercialized under the name *Forum World Features* (managed by the author of this chapter) and sold to subscribing newspapers in many countries (excluding the United States).

To deal with the secret or semisecret aspects of the cold war, though essential, is not sufficient. The full picture requires a look at the public events of the troubled postwar period. President Truman's second secretary of state—General George C. Marshall, who succeeded James Byrnes in January 1947—was that rarity, a high-ranking career officer who was also an admirable public servant in a democracy. His appointment was typical of the innate wisdom of the new leader, who lacked experience in international relations. Together, Truman and Marshall constituted a powerful team. Truman allowed Marshall a considerable latitude, while shouldering ultimate responsibility, well summed up by the legendary motto displayed on his desk in the Oval Office: The Buck Stops Here.

As mentioned earlier a real civil war was raging in 1946 in Greece, where the local communist guerrillas were annihilating anticommunist bands. Neighboring Turkey, too, felt itself under threat from the Soviet Union. With an ill-equipped army and a stagnant economy, the Turks were in no position to meet a threat from the Soviet Union. At this difficult stage, early in 1947, the British government suddenly informed the United States that British aid to Greece would shortly have to be cut off.

The president and General Marshall were convinced that

---

8. The author of this chapter was involved in both French initiatives, from 1958 with the Cinquième Bureaux and from 1970 with the SDECE.

the Soviet threat must be countered, as indeed were the armed forces. Marshall's number two, Dean Acheson (who would succeed him in 1949), put the challenge to Congress. Soviet pressure on the Dardanelles, on northern Greece, and on Iran, he said, had reached the point where three continents could be opened to communist penetration. As Acheson put it later:

Like apples in a barrel, infected by one rotten one, the corruption of Greece would infect Iran and all to the east. It would also carry infection to Africa through Asia Minor and Egypt and to Europe through Italy and France, already threatened by the strongest domestic Communist parties in western Europe.[9]

On March 12, 1947, President Truman addressed a joint session of Congress in a powerful speech enshrining the Truman Doctrine. "Should we fail to aid Greece and Turkey in this fateful hour," he said, "the effect will be far-reaching to the West as well as to the East. We must take immediate and resolute action."[10]

Truman's eloquence won the day but not immediately. Two months of congressional debate followed, and it was not until May 22 that the Greek-Turkish Aid Act was signed by the president. But this failed to keep communism at bay. The act was followed by the commitment to a U.S. naval presence in the eastern Mediterranean. Years later (in 1952) Greece and Turkey joined NATO and the American naval squadron was enlarged to become the Sixth Fleet.

Although the threats to Greece and Turkey were countered, a difficult challenge also arose in Iran. At Yalta, and again at Potsdam, Stalin had advanced claims to Iran as well

---

9. Middleton, *This War*, p. 69.
10. Ibid.

as to Turkey. During the war, British and Soviet forces had occupied Iranian territory in an effort to prevent a German occupation. Indeed, Iran had become one of the main supply routes for American aid to the Red Army in the later stages of World War II. Both powers agreed to withdraw their forces within six months of the end of hostilities. Britain complied but not the Soviet Union. On Stalin's orders, the Iranian Communist Party, which had styled itself the Tudeh ("Masses"), set up two separate states on the Soviet police model: the Autonomous Republic of Azerbaidjan and the Kurdish People's Republic.

In January 1946, Iran appealed to the United Nations Security Council. The appeal attracted unpleasant anti-Soviet reactions and a strongly anti-Soviet attitude from President Truman. Suddenly, and without seeking any further publicity, Stalin withdrew the Soviet forces from both Soviet-appointed "republics." Each survived the Soviet departure but not for long. Stalin showed no such compliance in the more ruthless occupation of the East European countries: Bulgaria, Albania, Romania, Hungary, Poland, Yugolavia, Austria, and East Germany.

The facts marshalled above make it clear why there was a cold war but leave unanswered a further question: Why did the cold war remain cold? The main reason, without a doubt in my mind, was the international balance of terror. At war's end, the United States was still the world's only atomic power and, of course, the only power that had used it, to end the war with Japan by its mass destruction of Hiroshima and Nagasaki. The A-bomb was followed by the awesome H-bomb, but in October 1961 the Soviet Union in effect caught up with the United States by successfully testing a fifty-plus-megaton hydrogen bomb in the Arctic.

Although it was never likely that the United States would

unilaterally use the H-bomb against the world's only other superpower, the Soviet success in this controversial sphere made a nuclear war even more unlikely than it had been during the relatively short period of U.S. monopoly. The only incident that threatened to spark a nuclear war was the confrontation between President John F.Kennedy and the Soviet leader Nikita Khrushchev during the Cuban missile crisis of 1962. It is worth recalling that, thanks to the solid and decisive evidence provided to the CIA by the pro-West double agent Oleg Penkovsky, Kennedy was able to stand up to the threat posed by Khrushchev in the knowledge that the Soviet leader was in no condition to outmatch the American president.[11] Thereafter, despite the antics of the international antinuclear groups, there was no real danger of a nuclear war.

COLD AND NOT SO COLD

Thus, the cold war between the two superpowers remained cold. It is important, however, to recall that Moscow fought several wars by proxy against the West. In other words, the Soviet Union, without committing its own forces, helped its ideological protégés wage wars in the spirit of Lenin's stated aim to carry communism to "all countries of the world without exception." One of these conflicts was the Korean War, which would not have happened if Stalin had not given a go-ahead to the North Korean leader, Kim Il Sung, who had gone to Moscow to ask Stalin's approval of his plan to invade South Korea. A major player in the war was communist China, which had also sought, and been given, Stalin's approval to aid

11. Jerrold L. Schecter and Peter S. Deriabin, *The Spy Who Saved the World: How a Soviet Colonel Changed the Course of the Cold War* (New York: Scribners, 1992).

North Korea. As it happened, the Soviet Union committed a major error of judgment at the crucial time; since January 1950, the Soviet representative on the United Nations Security Council, Jacob Malik, had been boycotting the proceedings because China's seat was still occupied by Taiwan. The Soviets were therefore unable to veto President Truman's moves to commit the United Nations (principally, of course, the United States) to defend South Korea against communist aggression. Without this error of judgment, North Korea would probably have defeated, and taken over, the South.

No such errors were committed before and during the two Indochina wars: against France, the colonial power (1945–54), and against the United States, the anticommunist superpower (1958–75). The most relevant fact, in the context of this chapter, is that both Indochina wars were launched by one of the leading figures in international communism: Ho Chi Minh, a founder-member of the French Communist Party who went on to Moscow for further training. The fact that Ho died before the United States withdrew from the war does not affect the issue.

Despite these and many other successes, two other incidents made it clear to Moscow that, for all the continuing lip service to Leninism, there was no way that the Soviet Union would "win" the cold war. The two issues were different in kind but of special relevance to each other in the context of the time. Both count as important victories to be credited to President Ronald Reagan. One was his decision in October 1983 to "invade" the Caribbean island of Grenada. The other was the launching of the Strategic Defense Initiative in the same year. A further strategic reverse, of still greater relevance to this chapter, was the Soviet decision to invade Afghanistan.

On March 11, 1979, the government of Grenada, headed by Sir Eric Gairey, was overthrown in an almost bloodless coup by Maurice Bishop, whose party, the New Jewel Movement, was communist in all but name. At twenty-one miles by twelve, Grenada was a Caribbean ministate and a member of the British Commonwealth. Between July 1980 and April 1983, Grenada signed agreements with the Soviet Union, Bulgaria, Czechoslovakia, and North Korea. Special relations were also developed between the ruling New Jewel Movement in Grenada and the Soviet Communist Party, as well as with the communist regime in Nicaragua.

On October 25, 1983, a U.S. force of 1,000 men landed on Grenada, shortly followed by a further 300-strong contingent. The stated purpose of the landings was to rescue 603 American medical students. The real reason was spelled out by President Reagan, who said, four days later (just after the miniwar had been won), that Grenada, far from being an "island paradise," was in fact "a Soviet-Cuban colony being readied for use as a major military bastion to export terror." He added, "We arrived just in time."

The real purpose of Reagan's Strategic Defense Initiative (SDI) was to demonstrate to the world in general, and the Soviet Union in particular, that the latter could no longer afford to compete with the United States in financing and producing high-technology weapons. It is important to realize that the purpose of SDI was purely defensive: the demonstrated ability to destroy enemy nuclear missiles in the stratosphere, before they could hit their targets. This purpose was, in effect, seriously misrepresented by whoever coined the alternative term, "Star Wars."

When the last Soviet troops pulled out of Afghanistan, in February 1989, after nearly ten years of war, it could be seen that this one war of aggression beyond the boundaries of the tsarist empire had ended in disaster for Moscow. Certainly, this major defeat can be seen as the decisive turning point in the Soviet Union's imperialist expansion.

The defense offered of the various Afghan resistance groups—spurred as much by Islamic fervor as by patriotism—had brought the invading Soviet forces and the official Afghan army to a standstill. For the first time, the "normal" techniques used by the Soviet Union had failed. With a high level of Soviet funding and intensive training of cadres by the KGB, the new, Soviet-backed Afghan security service—the Khad—had built up a force of 30,000, which had infiltrated the guerrillas and built up a big network of informers. Nevertheless, in the end the guerrillas won with significant military help from the United States, and the invaders pulled out.

Despite an immense, indeed unprecedented, publicity campaign by Mikhail Gorbachev, the Soviet system collapsed, bringing the cold war to an end.

9

Judgments and Misjudgments

Paul Hollander

TRENDS AND PATTERNS

The tenth anniversary of the removal of the Berlin Wall is a welcome opportunity not only to examine the historical significance of the fall of Soviet communism but also to reflect on Western assessments of communist systems.[1] Sad to say, Western views of these systems were more often than not mis-

Not even a modestly systematic sampling of the literature on communist systems is feasible in an essay of this length. I listed sources I quoted from or made specific reference to and a few others I wished to draw attention to—neglected or forgotten works deserving continued attention. I was also selective in mentioning the names of *some* who made important contributions to understanding (or misunderstanding) communist systems.

1. The communist systems to which reference is being made include the former Soviet Union and its "Socialist Commonwealth" in Eastern Europe plus Albania, China, Cuba, Vietnam, North Korea, and Nicaragua under the Sandinistas. Communist states in Africa such as Angola, Mozambique, and Ethiopia attracted lesser Western attention.

taken, both in their moral and their factual aspects, sometimes grotesquely and spectacularly so. To be sure these systems were secretive and far from welcoming inquiry into their character. Not only did they make it difficult for outside observers to learn about their institutions and the ways of life they created, but they invested huge resources in producing false impressions, facades of themselves. Despite these efforts there was sufficient if incomplete information to apprehend their essential characteristics; limited access to data was a less critical impediment to proper understanding than the predisposition of the observers.

I have had an almost lifelong interest in the Western views of communist systems and especially those among them I regarded as wrongheaded.[2] Although this preoccupation crystallized during my professional life in the West, its roots are to be found in my experiences in communist Hungary where I grew

2. The major product of this preoccupation has been *Political Pilgrims: Travel of Western Intellectuals to the Soviet Union, China and Cuba 1928–1978* (New York: Oxford University Press, 1981; New York: Harper Colophon, 1983; Lanham, Md.: University Press of America, 1990; New Brunswick N.J.: Transaction Publishers, 1998).

See also "The Pilgrimage to Nicaragua" (chap. 5) in *Anti-Americanism: Critiques at Home and Abroad* (New York: Oxford University Press, 1992; New Brunswick, N.J.: Transaction Publishers, 1995); "The Newest Political Pilgrims," *Commentary*, August 1985; "Political Tourism in Cuba and Nicaragua," *Society*, May–June 1986; "Socialist Prisons and Imprisoned Minds," *National Interest*, winter 1987; "Durable Misconceptions of the Soviet Union," in *The Survival of the Adversary Culture* (New Brunswick, N.J.: Transaction Publishers, 1988); "The Appeals of Revolutionary Violence: Latin American Guerillas and American Intellectuals," in M. Radu, ed., *Violence and the Latin American Revolutions* (New Brunswick, N.J.: Transaction Publishers, 1988); "Resisting the Lessons of History: How the Adversary Culture Responded to the Disintegration of Communism," *Orbis*, fall 1990; "Soviet Terror, American Amnesia," *National Interest*, May 2, 1994; "Intellectuals and the Collapse of Communism," *Quadrant*, October 1995; "Comparative Moral Reassessments of Nazism and Communism," *Partisan Review*, fall 1995; and "The Durable Significance of the Political Pilgrimages," *Society*, July–August 1997.

up. My interest in the Western views of communism originated in the collision between widespread Western academic-intellectual perceptions of these systems and my experiences in Hungary between 1945 and 1956. The discussion that follows focuses on the views and judgments of those who most readily made them available: prominent intellectuals, including academics, writers, journalists, opinion makers, some scientists, and members of the clergy. The pervasiveness and influence of these views is suggested by the fact that entire professional associations, as for example the Latin American Studies Association in the United States, have repeatedly taken official positions in support of political systems such as Castro's Cuba and Sandinista Nicaragua. The professional association of American anthropologists displayed similar sentiments on several occasions. In 1990 the Organization of American Historians defeated a motion (supported by one member!) that welcomed glasnost in Soviet historiography and expressed regret that the same organization "never protested the forced betrayal of the historians' responsibility to truth imposed upon Soviet and East European historians by their political leaders."[3] During the Vietnam War numerous other professional academic organizations were on record supporting North Vietnam and the Vietcong. It would require another essay, preferably a volume, to discuss in what manner these sentiments influenced American or Western policies toward communist states and public opinion.

The views here examined have a moral-ethical as well as factual-historical dimension, although the two are closely connected; people taking positions on important moral-political questions usually manage to find facts to support them. In

3. Wilcomb E. Washburn, *The Treason of Intellectuals* (Herndon, Va: Young America's Foundation, spring 1991), p. 18.

some instances the link between the factual and the moral-judgmental dimension is clear: if the standard of living declined, if more people were in detention (or killed) for political reasons than under the previous government; if life expectancy declined, rates of crime stayed high, and so forth, a less favorable or downright negative moral judgment of these systems would be rendered. On the other hand even agreed on factual matters may invite different interpretations. It is possible to acknowledge problematic facts without reaching unfavorable conclusions about the character of these systems if these facts are treated as temporary, epiphenomenal, or an acceptable price paid for other gains and benefits, especially if the future realization of desirable goals is allowed into the moral equation. Questionable aspects of these systems may thus be acknowledged on the basis of what Arthur Koestler called "the doctrine of unshaken foundations." He wrote: "Weaknesses, failures, even crimes of the Soviet bureaucracy are admitted but claimed to be more surface symptoms which do not affect the fundamentally progressive nature of the Soviet Union, guaranteed by the nationalization of the means of production and the abolition of the profit motive." This was a position taken, among many others, by E. H. Carr, the English historian of the Soviet Union. He wrote that "while it would be wrong to . . . condone the sufferings and the horrors inflicted on large sections of the Russian people . . . it would be idle to deny that the sum of human well-being and human opportunity in Russia today is immeasurably greater that it was fifty years ago."[4] Upton Sinclair said about the collectivization of Soviet agriculture: "May be it cost a million lives—may be it cost five

4. "Soviet Myths and Reality," in *The Yogi and the Commissar* (New York: Collier, 1961), pp. 123–24; E. H. Carr quoted in Ferdinand Mount, ed., *Communism* (Chicago: University of Chicago Press, 1992), p. 191.

million. . . . There has never been in human history a great social change without killing."[5] Sartre explained, "in reply to Albert Camus's criticism of Soviet labor camps. . . . 'Like you I find these camps intolerable, but I find equally intolerable the use made of them . . . in the bourgeois press.'"[6] This was an arresting example of the conviction that criticism of the communist systems, however well founded, must not be expressed in public since their enemies will exploit it. In the same spirit William Kunstler, the famous radical lawyer, averred that he did not "believe in public attacks on socialist countries where violations of human rights may occur."[7]

Ignorance or denial of facts often combined with dismissing their moral-ethical importance. Few Westerners knew exactly how many people perished, for example, as a result of the forced collectivization of agriculture in the Soviet Union or during the so-called Cultural Revolution in China. The apologists generally opted for smaller numbers while simultaneously upholding the necessity of such sacrifices for the sake of other, long-term benefits.

Sometimes social-scientific ambitions shaped Western views of communist systems. It was thought by some that the pursuit of factual knowledge and objectivity required an abstention from "value judgments" or "moralizing" as far as communist systems were concerned. The same considerations were not applied to Nazi Germany and other systems or movements on the right of the political spectrum, nor did they inform studies of Western democratic societies.

The misjudgments of communist systems encompassed

5. Sinclair in Upton Sinclair and Eugene Lyons, *Terror in Russia? Two Views* (New York, 1938), pp. 11, 12.
6. Mount, *Communism*, p. 166.
7. *Village Voice*, May 28, 1979, pp. 25–26.

explanations of their origin, their key characteristics, as well as anticipations of their durability. This is not to say that such views completely dominated either public or scholarly opinion; as will be shown below many observers were capable of insightful diagnosis and appropriate moral judgment of communist systems; they also succeeded without much difficulty to provide solid factual bases for their moral judgments.

This essay, while focusing on the specifics of the perceptions and judgments of communist systems, also seeks to explain some of the patterns and trends in these perceptions—especially those that were grossly distorted. It is more difficult to explain what enabled some commentators to see these systems with far greater clarity and reach conclusions that came to be vindicated by both historical events and authoritative voices in the communist societies themselves, including former leaders, major functionaries, and party intellectuals.

One may ask why does it matter—especially at a time when most of these systems are already defunct—who in the West were right or wrong about their character? It is my belief (probably shared by other contributors to this volume) that ideas, beliefs, and moral and political judgments are not "ephiphenomenal," that they matter especially when expressed by members of elite groups. Such judgments may influence the climate of opinion, government, and business policy and have an impact on the lives of human beings, sometimes millions of them.

It is of further interest, constituting a mystifying puzzle, how distinguished, inquisitive, and in some ways highly qualified individuals arrive at and hold over long periods of time with great confidence astonishingly wrongheaded judgments about political systems, movements, and ideologies even when evidence challenging such views is available.

The perceptions of communist systems did undergo

changes over time. During the early years of the cold war and the Korean War there was an apparent anticommunist consensus that failed to endure; by the late 1960s the public mood had begun to change and the anticommunism of the earlier cold war years came to be replaced by anti-anticommunism among many intellectuals and opinion makers, in part a delayed backlash against McCarthyism. Anti-anticommunists believed that anticommunism had little foundation in reality and amounted to a greater evil than communism and that, given the inequities of American and other Western societies, their citizens had no moral basis for making critical judgments of the communist ones.

More than any other event it was the Vietnam War and its destructive, inconclusive nature that undermined and discredited criticism of communist systems and stimulated sympathy toward those in the Third World. As Francois Furet observed, "what emerged from the protests . . . was a resurgence of illusions about the Communist world."[8] This was a new set of illusions about countries other than the Soviet Union.

The perceptions of the Soviet Union had changed earlier, following Stalin's death in 1953 and Khrushchev's revelations in 1956; there followed a loss of interest and a measure of disillusionment on the left; the new and supposedly more authentic revolutionary regimes of Mao and Castro were more appealing than the USSR. More moderate Soviet domestic policies under Khrushchev and Brezhnev also contributed to a decline of enthusiasm and interest. Adam Ulam observed that intellectuals who had earlier found "a certain morbid fascination in the puritanic and repressive aspects of the Soviet regime and also in its enormous outward self assurance" found

8. *The Passing of an Illusion* (Chicago: University of Chicago Press, 1999), p. 494.

less to admire "when this facade of self-assurance began to collapse . . . after the revelations about Stalin in 1956."[9]

Somewhat similar attitudes toward China emerged following its rapprochement with the United States under Nixon and its encouragment of private enterprise and consumption after the death of Mao. Interest in communist Vietnam too waned after it ceased to be engaged in war with the United States and began to encourage private enterprise and foreign investment. Communist Cambodia's short-lived attractions under Pol Pot vanished as soon as it became embroiled in war with another communist state, Vietnam, and the mass murders of the regime were attested to by another communist government, that of victorious Vietnam. It is worth recalling that before its war with Vietnam reports of the mass murders of the Pol Pol regime were dismissed and ridiculed by Noam Chomsky and Edward Herman; Richard Dudman, a journalist highly regarded by Chomsky, "did not find [in Cambodia] the grim picture painted by . . . refugees who couldn't take the new order."[10]

Despite the changes noted above there was a remarkable continuity and resilience in the basic perceptions of communist states over the better part of an entire century. Each new communist state came to be thought of as more authentic and virtuous than its predecessor and invested with the qualities the more discredited ones were supposed to possess at earlier times.

It is noteworthy that the most favorable assessments of the

9. "The 'Essential Love' of Simone de Beauvoir," *Problems of Communism*, March–April 1966, p. 63.

10. Noam Chomsky and Edward S. Herman, "Distortions at Fourth Hand," *Nation*, June 1977, pp. 789, 791, 792. See also by the same authors, *After the Cataclysm: Postwar Indochina and the Reconstruction of Imperial Ideology* (Boston: South End Press, 1979), esp. p. 290. Dudman was cited in *After the Cataclysm*, esp. pp. 147, 149.

Soviet Union prevailed during the early and mid-1930s, the period of the catastrophic collectivization, the famines, the Great Purge, the show trials, mass arrests and murders, and the consolidation of the compulsory cult of Stalin. Western observers were either unfamiliar with these developments or dismissed their significance in light of the perceived accomplishments of the regime. Before the 1939 Nazi-Soviet pact pro-Soviet attitudes were often based on the conviction that the USSR was the only principled foe of nazism.

During World War II, the USSR was romanticized as a valiant ally and the patriotism of the Soviet people was confused with support for the political system. In the 1970s, during the years of détente, the United States government, the mass media, and the peace movement discouraged criticism, fearful of harming the cause of peace or what was earlier called "peaceful coexistence."

In a somewhat corresponding manner Western intellectuals' admiration of communist China peaked during one of the most destructive and bloody chapters of its history: the Cultural Revolution of the late 1960s.

Sandinista Nicaragua was the last communist system to be idealized (partly as a victim of American imperialism), the final incarnation of the hopes on the left to find a new geographic location for socialism with a human face.

Of all the communist systems, extinct and surviving, Cuba has been the most successful in retaining its earlier appeals because of the survival in power of a revolutionary leader unwilling to compromise or moderate his policies and abandon his anticapitalist and anti-American attittude and rhetoric. However, the favorable views did not survive unscathed; the periodic exodus of refugees, the economic crises following the collapse of the Soviet bloc (leading to the cessation of Soviet aid), the evidence of growing domestic social problems (crime, prostitution, black marketeering), accepance of the dollar as quasi-official currency, all have made a dent on the favorable perceptions. Nonetheless it is still conventional wisdom in much of the media and among academic intellectuals that communist Cuba has done all it could to improve the material existence, health, and education of its citizens—a view the television critic Walter Goodman called "a portrait of Cuba without warts." As of 1994 Dr. Benjamin Spock was among those who continued to give every benefit of doubt to communist Cuba.[11] The remaining sympathizers blamed Cuba's difficulties on the United States.

In both the 1930s and later, during the 1960s and 1970s, Westerners' predisposition and receptivity toward communist systems were shaped by conditions and problems in their own society, including the changing views of tradition and modernity. In the Soviet Union of the 1930s, industrialization and urbanization made a highly favorable impression on sympathetic Western observers, as well as the alleged attitudinal liberation of society from the shackles of the past. (Typically, Louis Fisher rhapsodized about "steel and iron . . . vanquishing Russia's wood civilization."[12]) By contrast, during the 1960s and 1970s countries like communist China, Cuba, and Vietnam (and others in the Third World) were found appealing in part because they did not succumb to what was by then seen as the dehumanizing and depersonalizing processes associated with modernization. Harrison Salisbury was impressed in China by seeing "men and women [who] labored with their

11. Walter Goodman, New York Times, April 6, 1991. See Dr. Spock's letter in the New York Times, September 4, 1994. Carol Brightman, venerable admirer of Cuba and coeditor of the worshipful volume entitled Venceremos Brigade (New York, 1971), as of 1995 still considered critiques of Cuba "distortions" (letter, New York Times, November 9, 1995).

12. Men and Politics (New York: Duell, Sloane and Pierce, 1941), p. 189.

own hands, with a few animals, a few primitive implements—experiencing life so simple, so integrated with the land, the weather and the plants that its symmetry seemed almost magical."[13]

By the late 1960s many Western intellectuals and their followers were repulsed by many aspects of life linked to modernity: the decline of community, mass culture, urban crowding, bureaucracy, specialization, encroachments on nature, excessive consumption, and the loss of authenticity in personal relations. They were under the impression that the second generation of communist societies and their simple, good people (representing a new version of the noble savage) preserved some sort of a preindustrial authenticity and innocence; it was also believed that these systems would spare their physical environment from the ravages of industrialization and urbanization; that they were not wasteful; they did not consume mindlessly, were not competitive, and were led by kindly, caring leaders.

Another trend during the 1960s and 1970s that influenced the perception of communist states and especially the USSR was the "convergence theory"—amounting to the belief that similar levels of industrial development will lead to similar political structures and practices, and hence a more developed Soviet Union (and other more industrialized communist countries) will become more democratic and tolerant.

A less benign version of the convergence theory that also emerged during the late 1960s, stimulated by the alienation the Vietnam War inspired and reinforced, was that of moral equivalence, the conviction (rapidly becoming conventional wisdom among much of the intelligentsia) that the United States was in no way superior or preferable to the Soviet Union

---

13. *To Peking and Beyond* (New York: Quadrangle, 1973), pp. 73–74.

or that capitalism was in no way superior to state socialism. The Soviet Union was no longer idealized but was still viewed far less critically. The moral equivalence approach sought to discredit the United States by equating its flaws with those of the Soviet Union but at the same time judged the Soviet Union more leniently as being no worse than the United States!

Another by-product of the 1960s was the revisionist school of Soviet historiography, which also grew out at least in part of the anti-American animus stimulated by the Vietnam War. It had three major thrusts. One was the insistence that the United States and the West had a greater share of responsibility for the cold war and arms race than the USSR; second was the denial that the Soviet Union was, or had ever been, a totalitarian society; the third was the reinterpretation of the purges, including the (downward) revision of the number of its victims and questioning Stalin's responsibility. On the one hand the revisionists reconceptualized the purges and the associated mass killings as localized, uncoordinated events and on the other as largely administrative proceedings providing new opportunities for social mobility.[14]

A final stage in the evolution of Western views of the Soviet Union occurred during the Gorbachev era, which inspired hopes among some intellectuals that the Soviet Union might yet reclaim its founding ideals and become at last a democratic socialist society.[15]

14. See, for example, J. Arch Getty, *Origins of the Great Purges* (New York: Cambridge University Press, 1985); Getty and Roberta T. Manning, eds., *Stalinist Terror: New Perspectives* (New York: Cambridge University Press, 1993); Robert V. Thurston, *Life and Terror in Stalin's Russia 1934–1941* (New Haven, Conn.: Yale University Press, 1996). Revisionist (and nonjudgmental) views of Stalin and Soviet history may also be founds in the work of Theodore von Laue.

15. Stephen F. Cohen wrote: "The emergence of a Soviet leadership devoted to radical reform confounded most Western scholars . . . who had long

One more interesting change in the assessments of these systems over time may be noted here. Before the collapse sympathizers believed that these regimes were guided by the insights and propositions of Marxism, which was a great source of their strength and attraction. Since their demise many former supporters have argued—to salvage the theory from becoming historically compromised and tainted—that these systems had never been true to Marxism but fradulently claimed to be inspired by it.

PREDICTIONS OF DURABILITY

Few Western scholars, intellectuals, government officials, or politicians predicted the collapse of Soviet communism. Riszard Kapuscinski, the Polish author, observed that "just before the breakup of the USSR, the view of that country as a model of the most stable and durable system in the world had gained wide acceptance among Western Sovietologists."[16] Robert M. Gates, former head of the CIA, confessed that "he was amazed by the breakdown of the USSR and rests his defense on the entirely fair observation that virtually no one in the defense or intelligence business predicted that the Soviet Union was bound for the dustbin of history until it hit bottom."[17] Walter Laqueur reminded us (following the collapse) that "the general view in the West during most of the 1960s and 1970s was that the Soviet Union had no monopoly on

---

believed that the Soviet communist system lacked any capacity for real change." Apparently Cohen believed otherwise (Stephen P. Cohen and Katrina vanden Heuvel, eds., *Voices of Glasnost* [New York: Norton, 1989], p. 14).

16. *Imperium* (New York: Knopf, 1994), p. 314.

17. Quoted in Thomas Powers, "Who Won the Cold War?" *New York Review of Books*, June 20, 1996, p. 20.

serious economic problems, which seemed by no means incurable. . . . With a few exceptions Western experts grossly overrated the Soviet GNP and thus underrated per capita arms spending and thus the defense burden for the population. . . . According to a study published as late as 1988 by a well-known Western economist [E. A.Hewett] specializing in the Soviet Union, Soviet citizens enjoyed 'massive economic security.'"[18] Seweryn Bialer, wrote in 1982 that "the Soviet economy . . . administered by intelligent and trained professionals will not go bankrupt . . . like the political system, it will not collapse."[19] Jerry Hough, another prominent Soviet specialist, argued in 1991 that "economic reform in the Soviet Union was going ahead with amazing speed and that Soviet political problems had been grossly exaggerated." He also wrote shortly before the historical events of the summer and fall of 1991: "The belief that the Soviet Union may disintegrate as a country contradicts all we know about revolution and national integration throughout the world. . . . Anyone who sees him [Gorbachev] as a tragic transitional figure has little sense of history."[20] Moshe Lewin, the historian, saw in 1988 the Soviet Communist Party as "the main stabilizer of the political system" and could not conceive of conditions under which any group "would back measures likely to erode the integrity of the entire union or the centralised state. The party . . . is the only institution that can preside over the overhaul of the system."[21]

It is clear in retrospect that both Western specialists and

18. *The Dream That Failed: Reflections on the Soviet Union* (New York: Oxford University Press, 1994), pp. 57, 59, 99.

19. Quoted in *Freedom Review*, July–August 1992, p. 7.

20. Quoted in Laqueur, *The Dream That Failed*, pp. 120, 211.

21. *The Gorbachev Phenomenon* (Berkeley: University of California Press, 1988), pp. 131, 133.

Western political elites were susceptible to the impressions of strength and stability the regime projected, often by means of crude propaganda succeeding to cover up or distract attention from its underlying weaknesses. Martin Malia wrote in 1990 that "the world in fact was being hoodwinked by the assertion of efficacy and power in just one domain" (i.e., heavy industry and military production).[22] John Lewis Gaddis noted that "nuclear weapons preserved the image of a formidable Soviet Union long after it had entered into its terminal decline."[23]

Senator Daniel Patrick Moynihan was among the handful who envisioned the eventual disintegration of the Soviet Union not merely on economic grounds but from a more profound malaise of the entire system. Robert Conquest wrote as early as in 1969 that "in the long run the system is not only inhuman but also unsuccessful, and crisis is not an accidental but necessary result." Richard Pipes was another observer who had few illusions about the long-term stability of the Soviet system, noting as of 1984 that it was in a "crisis" and "has outlived its usefulness and that the forces making for change are becoming well-nigh irresistible."[24]

Why was it so widely believed that the Soviet Union was virtually indestructible? Seymour Martin Lipset and Gyorgy Bence observed that, by the 1970s and 1980s, "most of the Sovietologists . . . were left-liberal in their politics, an orientation that undermined their capacity to accept the view that

22. Quoted in William M. Brinton and Alan Rinzler, eds., *Without Force or Lies* (San Francisco: Mercury House, 1990), p. 405.

23. *We Now Know: Rethinking Cold War History* (Oxford, U.K., 1997), pp. 292, 222.

24. Moynihan in *Newsweek*, November 19, 1979, pp. 136, 141; Conquest in *New York Times Magazine*, August 18, 1969; Pipes in *Foreign Affairs*, fall 1984, pp. 50, 60.

economic statism, planning, socialist incentives, would not work."[25]

Of all the reasons for the Western failure to anticipate the unraveling of the Soviet empire, the beliefs in the superpower symmetry and moral equivalence were probably the most important. It was widely held that global stability required an equilibrium between these powers. Critical views of the United States were anchored in the seemingly objective equation of its shortcomings with those of the Soviet Union; the somewhat cynical, hence apparently impartial, wisdom used to be that neither of the superpowers inspired much respect and that each used the alleged threat from the other for various amoral purposes (including bloated defense budgets). Even when the domestic weaknesses of the Soviet Union were noted, its successes abroad seemed impressive, especially its spreading influence in the Third World.[26]

Another important force contributing to the Western belief in the durability of the Soviet Union was the antinuclear/ peace movement. All those convinced of the imminence of nuclear holocaust who dedicated their lives, or at least their public lives, to averting the disaster had a vested interest in the persistence of the Soviet Union. The peace movement could not flourish without the cold war.

There were also those who were deeply (and hopefully) committed to the idea that the "late capitalist" United States was in terminal decline, the most decadent society in existence. In this view American decadence was caused by, or associated, with the ills and evils of capitalism; a socialist (even

25. "Anticipations of the Failure of Communism," *Theory and Society*, no. 23 (1994): 202.
26. See, for example, Alvin Z. Rubinstein, "Soviet Success Story: The Third World," *Orbis*, fall 1988.

a semi- or quasi-socialist) society such as the USSR was expected to have a greater staying power and a better chance to solve its problems. Even as "actually existing socialism" was in the process of collapsing in the Soviet Union and Eastern Europe, some American intellectuals entertained hopes of its rebirth.[27]

There were also critics of the United States (at home and abroad) who believed that the Soviet Union was a critical counterweight to the predatory imperialism of the United States and did not wish to contemplate a world without it. Such wishful thinking also contributed to a belief in the durability of the USSR.

With few exceptions (such as noted above) the critics of the Soviet system were no more capable of predicting its end than those less averse to its prolonged existence. The "cold warriors" and unembarrassed critics of the Soviet Union (among them this writer) had few illusions about the advantages of Soviet socialism over the alleged depravities of capitalism and were not tempted to consider the Soviet Union a successful modernizing society. Their belief in the durability of the Soviet system did not derive from overlooking its profound moral, political, or economic flaws; they were not under the impression that it had enjoyed a high degree of legitimacy despite its shortcomings (as many on the left believed); they did not believe that there was an implicit "social contract" between the rulers and the ruled. The anticommunist critics thought that the system was durable because, it seemed to

---

27. Bertell Ollman wrote: "Paradoxically enough, the objective conditions for socialism in the USSR are now largely present, but because of the unhappy experience with a regime that called itself 'socialist' the subjective conditions are absent. . . . On the other hand . . . the Soviet Union might be saved by a socialist revolution in the West as our capitalist economy goes into a tailspin" (*PS: Political Science and Politics*, September 1991, p. 460).

thcm (wrongly, as it turned out), it had succeeded in building institutions of control that would keep it going regardless of economic inefficiency and limited or minimal legitimacy, and because the USSR managed to offset domestic stagnation by expansion abroad and by preserving its status as superpower.

In retrospect it is clear that the anticommunist critics had overestimated the efficiency of the apparatus of control, the political cohesion of the ruling elite, and its ability to manipulate the citizenry regardless of its growing discontents. The critics also underestimated the long-term subversive impact of increased information about and contact with the West that began in the 1970s. Their views were influenced by the theory of totalitarianism, which used to be helpful for grasping the character of the Soviet system but failed to stimulate anticipations of its end.

FANTASIES AND PROJECTIONS

Regardless of the location, historical background, or stage of development of the various communist states, their misapprehensions had much in common because they had similar origins, mainly the desire to find alternatives to what many Westerners considered their own unjust social systems. More recently it was the deepening problems of secular modernity that created receptivity to societies that claimed to have found ways to deal with them effectively. The misperceptions grew out of the recurring desire of people (at once highly individualistic and longing for a sense of purpose and community) to escape social isolation and lack of meaning.

The communist states were often envisioned by sympathetic Western intellectuals as heirs to the goals and traditions of the Enlightenment, progress, or a humane socialism. Graham Greene wrote in 1967: "If I had to choose between life in the Soviet Union and life in the United States I would certainly choose the Soviet Union."[28] Georg Lukacs in 1971 said, in the face of much disconfirming evidence he possessed: "I have always thought that the worst form of socialism is better to live in than the best form of capitalism."[29] During the Vietnam War Tom Hayden and Staughton Lynd wrote: "we felt empathy for . . . spokesmen for the Communist world in Prague and Moscow, Peking and Hanoi. After all, we call ourselves in some sense revolutionaries. So do they. After all we identify with the poor and oppressed. So do they."[30]

The wishful misperceptions of communist systems peaked at periods when Western societies faced serious internal problems: the economic crises of the late 1920s and early 1930s and the political-cultural ones of the 1960s and early 1970s. In the former period only one communist system existed, the Soviet Union; in the latter there were several, and they eclipsed a USSR tarnished not only by Khrushchev's revelations in 1956 but also by the Soviet repression of the Hungarian Revolution of 1956 and of the Czech attempt in 1968 to humanize Soviet-style socialism.

Western misconceptions of communist countries were shaped by ignorance, wishful thinking, favorable predisposition, and sometimes the manipulation of impressions and experiences (in the case of visitors taken on elaborate conducted tours). Ignorance was nurtured by a determination to overlook information that could have cast doubt on the favorable predisposition, for example, the published recollections of former

28. Letter, *Times* (London), September 4, 1967.
29. Francois Furet, *The Passing of an Illusion* (Chicago: University of Chicago Press, 1999), p. 117.
30. *The Other Side* (New York: New American Library, 1966), pp. 17–18.

residents of communist states. Often scholars too ignored such information, regarding it as biased.

Major facts of life in these countries thus remained unfamiliar and sometimes incomprehensible. They often included the standards of living of ordinary citizens, the wastefulness and inefficiency of the "planned" economy, the prevailing levels of intimidation, the treatment of political prisoners, the staging of political trials, the travel restrictions combined with the internal passport system, the privileges of the party and government elite, the enormity of corruption, the mendaciousness of the official propaganda.

Julian Huxley, the British scientist, sincerely believed in 1932 that in the Soviet Union the "level of physique and general health [was] rather above that to be seen in England."[31] George Bernard Shaw, looking around an elegant restaurant in Moscow in 1931, dismissed the possibility of food shortages in the country at large, whereas John Kenneth Galbraith—on his tour of communist China, after having been shown the kitchen of a plant—concluded that "if there is any shortage of food it was not evident in the kitchen."[32] Billy Graham found "no evidence of religious repression" in the Soviet Union but was greatly impressed by the provisions he received, noting that "the meals I had are among the best I have ever eaten. . . . In the United States you have to be a millionaire to have caviar, but I had caviar with almost every meal."[33]

Spiritual nourishment was also highly rated. It was widely

31. *A Scientist among the Soviets* (London: Harper Brothers, 1932), p. 67.
32. Eugene Lyons, *Assignement in Utopia* (London: Harcourt Brace, 1938), p. 430; *China Passage* (Boston: Houghton Mifflin, 1973), p. 54.
33. "Graham Offers Positive Views of Religion in Soviet," *New York Times*, May 13, 1982; "Billy Graham Rebutts Criticism of Soviet Trip," *New York Times*, May 18, 1982; and "Billy Graham Back Home, Defends Remarks," *New York Times*, May 20, 1982.

believed that a sense of purpose and community permeated and animated communist societies and that the conflict between the private and public, the personal and social, had been abolished or was in the process of extinction. The Soviet system, according to Malcolm Cowley, the Amerian writer, "was capable of supplying the moral qualities that writers missed in bourgeois society: the comradeship in struggle, the self-imposed discipline, the ultimate purpose . . . the opportunity for heroism and human dignity."[34] Leon Feuchtwanger, the German writer, rejoiced in the "invigorating atmosphere" of the Soviet Union where he found "clarity and resolution."[35] John Dewey compared the ethos prevailing in the Soviet Union to "the moving spirit and force of primitive Christianity,"[36] and Edmund Wilson confessed that "you feel in the Soviet Union that you are on the moral top of the world where the light never really goes out."[37] J. D. Bernal, the British scientist, found "sense of purpose and achievement" and was persuaded that "the cornerstone of the [Soviet] Marxist state was the utilization of human knowledge, science and technique, directly for hman welfare."[38] Anna Louise Strong observed that the "remaking of criminals is only one specialized form of the process of remaking human beings which goes on . . . in the Soviet Union."[39]

In Mao's China David Rockefeller found "a sense of na-

34. *Dream of the Golden Mountains* (New York: Viking, 1980), p. 43.

35. *Moscow 1937* (London: Gollancz, 1937), pp. 149–50.

36. *John Dewey: Impressions of Soviet Russia and the Revolutionary World* (New York: Bureau of Publications, Teachers College, Columbia University, 1929), p. 105.

37. *Travels in Two Democracies* (New York: Harcourt Brace, 1936), p. 321.

38. Quoted in Gary Wersky, *The Visible College* (New York: Holt, Rinehart and Winston, 1979), pp. 148, 193.

39. *This Soviet World* (New York, 1936), p. 250.

tional harmony . . . high morale and community of purpose
. . . crime, drug addiction, prostitution and venereal diseases
have been virtually eliminated. Doors are routinely left un-
locked." Felix Greene, the British author, reported that "China
is today an intensely . . . 'moral' society."[40] John K. Fairbank,
the widely respected Sinologist, was convinced in 1972 that
"the Maoist Revolution is . . . the best thing that happened to
the Chinese people in centuries."[41] Jan Myrdal believed that
China was held together by "discussions of Mao's thoughts."[42]

Saul Landau claimed that Cuba under Castro "is the first
purposeful society that we had in the Western hemisphere for
many years . . . the first society where . . . men have a certain
dignity, and where this is guaranteed to them."[43] C. Wright
Mills, the sociologist and merciless critic of American society,
was swept off his feet by the charms of Castro and revolutionary Cuba.[44] A publication of the National Council of Churches
informed the reader that "permeating the Cuban educational
practice is the concept that a new type of society will develop
a new type of human being . . . bound to others by solidarity,
comradeship and love."[45] As for Vietnam, Susan Sontag observed that "the phenomenon of existential agony, of alienation just don't appear among the Vietnamese," they are
"'whole' human beings not 'split' as we are."[46] John Brentlin-

40. "From a China Traveler," *New York Times*, August 10, 1973; Felix
Green, *Awakened China* (New York: Doubleday, 1961), p. 157.

41. "The New China and the American Connection," *Foreign Affairs*,
October 1972, pp. 31, 36.

42. Jan Myrdal with Gun Kessle, *The Revolution Continued* (New York:
Pantheon, 1970), p. 191.

43. "Cuba: The Present Reality," *New Left Review*, May–June 1961, p.
22.

44. *Listen Yankee* (New York: McGraw-Hill, 1960).

45. Quoted in Joshua Muravchik, "Pliant Protestants," *New Republic*,
June 13, 1983.

46. *Trip to Hanoi* (New York: Farrar, Straus and Giroux, 1968), pp. 69, 77.

ger, a professor of philosphy, found Sandinista Nicaragua "a deeply spiritual country trying to . . . build a new version of socialism." The officials he met were "dedicated, intense . . . willing to admit mistakes . . . but insistent concerning their good intentions and the progress the revolution was making."[47] Günter Grass, the famous German writer, escorted around Nicaragua by Tomas Borges, head of state security, reached the conclusion that in Sandinista Nicaragua "Christ's words are taken literally."[48] Harold Pinter, the playwright, compared Soviet intervention in Czechoslovakia in 1968 to American attempts to overthrow the government of Nicaragua and was persuaded that the latter "set out to establish a stable and decent society." Noam Chomsky suggested that the laudable social reforms of the Sandinistas could have had a subversive effect in Central America, "perhaps even the United States," which is why the United States sought to destroy the system.[49]

Plain or profound ignorance may also explain some of the Western perceptions of the Moscow trials in the 1930s as well as those in Eastern Europe after World War II.[50] Joseph Davies, U.S. ambassador to the USSR, and Walter Duranty, *New York Times* correspondent stationed in Moscow for many years, did not have the slightest doubt about the authenticity of these proceedings. Davies believed that Bukharin's guilt was estab-

47. *The Best of What We Are: Reflections on the Nicaraguan Revolution* (Amherst: University of Massachusetts Press, 1995), pp. 42, 36.

48. Quoted in Martin Diskin, ed., *Trouble in Our Backyard* (New York: Pantheon, 1983), p. 247.

49. *Contentions* (New York, September 1990), pp. 1–2; Noam Chomsky, *On Power and Ideology, Managua Lectures* (Boston: South End Press, 1987), pp. 38–39.

50. On the French intellectuals' perception of the post–World War II trials, see Tony Judt, *Past Imperfect: French Intellectuals 1944–1956* (Berkeley: University of California Press, 1992).

lished "beyond reasonable doubt," that the purges "cleansed the country," and that Vyshinsky, the vituperative prosecutor, "conducted the case with admirable moderation."[51] Duranty averred that "it is unthinkable that Stalin . . . and the Court Martial could have sentenced their friends to death unless the proofs of their guilt were overwhelming."[52] Henri Barbusse, Bertolt Brecht, and Upton Sinclair too considered these proceedings authentic and just.[53] Andre Malraux concluded with relief that, "just as the Inquisition did not affect the fundamental dignity of Christianity, so the Moscow trials have not diminished the fundamental dignity of communism."[54] Julien Benda (who had instructed intellectuals on how to avoid behavior incompatible with their lofty vocation) visited communist Hungary in 1949 to dispel French misconceptions about the innocence of Laszlo Rajk, the key defendant and victim of the Hungarian show trials after World War II.[55]

A combination of ignorance and wishful thinking might have prompted Sidney and Beatrice Webb to remark that Soviet prisons were "as free of physical cruelty as any prison in any country is ever likely to be."[56] G. B. Shaw and Anna Louise Strong, respectively, inclined to the opinion that Soviet and Chinese prisons were so humane and comfortable that inmates were reluctant to leave them on the expiration of their

51. *Mission to Moscow* (New York: Simon and Schuster, 1941), pp. 163, 168–69, 25.

52. *The Kremlin and the People* (New York: Reynold and Hitchcock, 1941), p. 65.

53. Quoted in Paul Hollander, *Political Pilgrims* (New York: Oxford University Press, 1981), pp. 161–63.

54. Jean Lacouture, *Andre Malraux* (New York: Pantheon, 1975), p. 230.

55. Gyorgy Faludi, *Pokolbeli Vig Napjaim* (My happy days in hell) (Budapest, 1989), pp. 313–15.

56. *Soviet Communism: A New Civilization?* (New York: Longman Green, 1935), p. 588.

sentences and that sometimes people applied for admission.[57] Henry Wallace (accompanied by Owen Lattimore) on a conducted tour of Soviet labor camps in the Kolyma region (properly described by Robert Conquest as the "Arctic death camps") was most favorably impressed by what he saw (including the camp commander), perceiving these camps as a combination of the Hudson Bay Company and Tennessee Valley Authority.[58] More recently Robert Thurston, an American historian, allowed that the inmates of the Gulag were not treated fairly by "Western standards of justice" but was comforted by the fact that in 1937 they had the opportunity to buy Soviet bonds, "an indication that they were still regarded as participants in society to some degree." A reviewer of his book noted that, "by this curious standard, sheep being led to slaughter are participants in agriculture."[59] Simone de Beauvoir was under the impression that "no administrative internment exist[ed] in China."[60] Basil Davidson, an English Africanist, after visiting what undoubtedly were model prisons, reached the conclusion that in China those sentenced for counterrevolutionary violence were better treated than violent criminals in Britain.[61] A report on Cuban prisons published by the Institute for Policy Studies in Washington, D.C., commented on the "strong sense of mission in most prison officials . . . [who] expressed great faith in their system and . . . seemed determined to work increasingly on their plan for reeducation. . . . We heard no complaints about . . . torture . . .

57. *Rationalization of Russia* (Bloomington: Indiana University Press, 1964), p. 91; *This Soviet World* (New York, 1936), p. 262.

58. Henry Wallace, *Soviet Asia Mission* (New York: Reynold and Hitchcock, 1946), pp. 33–35, 84, 217.

59. *New York Times Book Review*, May 1996, p. 14.

60. *The Long March* (Cleveland and New York: World, 1958), p. 388.

61. *Daybreak in China* (London: Cape, 1953), p. 183.

neither did we find any policy of extrajudicial executions or disappearances."[62] Salman Rushdie found Nicargua's constitution "amounting to a Bill of Rights I wouldn't have minded having on the statute book in Britain."[63]

Particular leaders were also often grotesquely misperceived, among them Stalin, Mao, Castro, Che Guevara, Ho Chi Minh, and the "commandantes" of Nicaragua. Sidney and Beatrice Webb considered Stalin "the duly elected representative of one of the Moscow constituencies to the Supreme Soviet . . . accountable to the representative assembly for all his activities."[64] Anna Louise Strong was reminded by "Stalin's method of running a committee . . . of Jane Addams . . . or Lillian D. Wald. . . . They had the same kind of democratically efficient technique, but they used more high pressure than Stalin did."[65] Ambassador Joseph Davies observed that Stalin's eyes were "exceedingly wise and gentle. A child would like to sit on his lap and a dog would sidle up to him."[66] Franklin D. Roosevelt, no starry-eyed intellectual, "after his return from Yalta . . . described Stalin to his cabinet as having 'something else in his being besides this revolutionist, Bolshevik thing' . . . this might have something to do with Stalin's earlier training for the 'priesthood.' . . . 'I think that something entered into his nature of the way in which a Christian gentleman should behave.'"[67] Hewlett Johnson, the dean of Canterbury

62. "Cuban Prisons: A Preliminary Report," IPS *Social Justice*, summer 1988, pp. 58, 59.
63. *The Jaguar Smile: A Nicaraguan Journey* (New York: Pan Books; London: Cape, 1987), p. 32.
64. *The Truth about Soviet Russia* (London: Longmans, 1942), pp. 16, 18.
65. Quoted in Stephen J. Whitfield, *Scott Nearing: Apostle of American Radicalism* (New York: Columbia University Press, 1974), p. 185.
66. *Mission to Moscow* (New York, 1943), p. 217.
67. Robert Nisbet, *The Failed Friendship* (Washington, D.C.: Regnery, 1988), pp. 11, 12.

(also an ardent admirer of the Soviet Union under Stalin and Stalin himself), discerned in Mao "an inexpressible look of kindness and sympathy, an obvious preoccupation with the needs of others."[68]

Sartre was overcome with admiration of Castro and Che Guevara, perceiving them as heroic figures who dispensed with sleep and other routine activities of lesser humans, "exercise[d] a veritable dictatorship over their own needs . . . [and] roll[ed] back the limits of the possible." Saul Landau saw Castro as "a man . . . steeped in democracy . . . a humble man."[69] A high-ranking official of the Swedish Social Democratic Party, Pierre Schori, compared Castro to a Renaissance prince.[70] Che Guevara reminded I. F Stone of Jesus: "In Che, one felt a desire to heal and pity for suffering . . . he was like an early saint."[71] Former president Carter on his goodwill visit to North Korea, according to a press report, "heaped praise on Kim Il Sung . . . 'I found him to be vigorous, intelligent, well informed . . . and in charge of decisions about his country.'" The short visit also allowed him to note "the reverence with which they [the North Korean people] look upon their leader."[72]

The favorable views of communist systems were largely based on imaginative projections of the hopes, ideals, and fantasies of Westerners persuaded that their notions of what

68. *China's New Creative Age* (New York: International Publishers, 1953), p. 153.
69. *Sartre on Cuba* (New York: Ballantine Books, 1961), pp. 102–3; Saul Landau, "Cuba: The Present Reality," *New Left Review*, May–June 1961, p. 15.
70. Per Ahlmark, *Tyranny and the Left, a Summary* (pamphlet based on book not available in English) (Stockholm, 1995), p. 28.
71. "The Legacy of Che Guevara," *Ramparts*, December 1967, pp. 20–21.
72. George Will, "Carter Misreads North Korea's Kim," *Daily Hampshire Gazette*, June 24, 1994.

makes a good society and exemplary ways of life were being realized in these countries. Thus devout religious believers (among them ministers, priests, and bishops) succeeded in persuading themselves that communist states respected religion and, despite their rhetoric, realized the essential precepts of Christianity. (Hewlett Johnson considered Soviet policies "singularly Christian" and "Russia . . . the most moral land I know. . . . During many months in Russsia . . . I never saw a sight I would screen from the eyes of a young girl."[73]) The pacifists managed to overlook communist militarism (later on, the unilateral disarmers, the Soviet nuclear arsenal), environmentalists, the destruction of the natural environment, populist antielitists, the vast power of the leaders. Of this phenomenon Malcolm Muggeridge wrote:

> There were earnest advocates of the humane killing of cattle who looked up at the massive headguarters of the OGPU [the political police] with tears of gratitude in their eyes, earnest advocates of proportional representation who eagerly assented when the necessity of the Dictatorship of the Proletariat was explained to them, earnest clergymen who walked reverently through anti-God museums . . . earnest pacifists who watched delightedly tanks rattle across Red Square . . . earnest town-planning specialists who stood outside overcrowded ramshackle tenements and muttered: "If only we had something like this in England!"[74]

Eugene Lyons remarked that the Soviet tourist agency sold "the glories of mass production to . . . California back-to-nature, handloom fadists. Vegetarians . . . swooned in ecstasy of admiration of Soviet slaughterhouses."[75] Phenomena deplored

73. *Soviet Power* (New York: International Publishers, 1940), p. 5; *Russia since the War* (New York: Boni and Gaer, 1947), p. 89.
74. *Chronicles of Wasted Time* (London: Collins, 1973), p. 244.
75. Lyons, *Assignment in Utopia*, p. 329.

under capitalism were reconceptualized and celebrated under communism. Beatrice and Sidney Webb were impressed by the higher purpose they associated with ordinary physical structures: "The marvel was not that there should be parks, hospitals, factories; after all these could be found in England as well. The marvel was that they should all, as the Webbs thought, be inspired by a collective ideal, a single moral purpose."[76] Koestler wrote of the same phenomenon: "For the addict of the Soviet myth the Dnieper Dam, the [Moscow] underground . . . Soviet aviation and Soviet flame-throwers assumed the fetish-character of a lock from the hair of the beloved."[77] Waldo Frank, the American writer, rhapsodized about a humane Russian locomotive.[78] Pablo Neruda found a visit to a Soviet hydroeletric plant unforgettable and described it as "the temple beside the lake."[79] American feminists in a Cuban nightclub found nothing wrong "with a woman showing her body and moving it on stage."[80] Simone de Beauvoir decided that pedicabs in communist China—unlike under capitalism—were not degrading.[81] Jonathan Kozol, the American social critic, was under the impression that Cubans didn't mind standing in lines: "The long lines . . . the ration cards and other forms of deprivation do not seem to dampen the high spirits of most people."[82] André Gide too believed, before the drastic revision of his views about the Soviet system, that Russians liked to

76. Gertrude Himmelfarb, "The Intellectual in Politics: The Case of the Webbs," *Journal of Contemporary History*, no. 3 (1971): 11.

77. Koestler, "Soviet Myths and Reality," p. 130.

78. *Dawn in Russia* (New York: Scribner, 1932), pp. 121, 127.

79. *Memoirs* (New York: Farrar, Straus and Giroux, 1977), p. 243.

80. Ronald Radosh, ed., *The New Cuba* (New York: Morrow, 1976), pp. 64–65.

81. Beauvoir, *The Long March*, p. 49.

82. *Children of the Revolution: A Yankee Teacher in Cuban Schools* (New York: Delacorte Press, 1978), p. 102.

stand in line.[83] John Kenneth Galbraith came to the conclusion that the Chinese system under Mao "was remarkably efficient" in distributing consumer goods.[84]

More recently John Mack (professor of psychiatry at Harvard Medical School) offered a benign interpretation of the withholding of information about the Chernobyl disaster as part of the "tendency on the part of Soviet authorities to downplay catastrophes and instead offer reassurance to the Soviet people so as to prevent emotional distress."[85] Perhaps not coincidentally, he was the same author who expressed a firm belief (in a book devoted to the topic) in extraterrestrial visitors.

The prestige of Marxism, supposedly guiding and legitimating the policies of communist systems, played a part in the positive assessments of academic intellectuals who believed that communist societies were shaped by this "science of society," by "scientific socialism." On closer inspection the attractions of Marxism appeared to be less than fully rational. Leszek Kolakowski wrote: "Marxism has been the greatest fantasy of our century. It was a dream offering the prospect of a society of perfect unity, in which all human aspirations would be fulfilled and all values reconciled. . . . The influence that Marxism achieved, far from being the result of its scientific character, is almost entirely due to its prophetic, fantastic and irrational elements."[86]

Thus the favorable assessments of these systems were

83. *Return from the USSR* (New York: McGraw-Hill, 1964), pp. 17–18.

84. Galbraith, *China Passage*, pp. 104, 115.

85. "Soviet Minds Sheltered from Catastrophe," letter, *New York Times*, May 15, 1986.

86. *Main Currents of Marxism*, vol. 3. (New York: Oxford University Press, 1978), pp. 523, 525. See also John Gray in Mount, *Communism*, p. 231.

more closely related to their stated objectives, ideals, and in tentions than their actual accomplishments, although the latter were also highly praised and vastly overrated. Even when sympahetic observers noted troubling matters—discrepancies between ends and accomplishments, costs and benefits, or ends and means—they succeeded in reassuring themselves by the grandeur of the goals and the historically unique vision the systems pursued.

E. J. Hobsbawm argued that "the Communist intellectual [in the West, that is], in opting for the USSR and his [communist] party did so because on balance the good on his side seemed to outweigh the bad." For these intellectuals (including Hobsbawm himself) the overriding, axiomatic "badness" was capitalism and the evils associated with it. Hobsbawm also wrote (rather self-servingly since he himself shared these attitudes as a lifelong sympathizer with communist movements and states) that "modern political choice is not a constant process of selecting men or measures, but a single or infrequent choice between packages, in which we buy the disagreeable part of the contents because there is no other way to be politically effective."[87] He did not explain how overlooking "disagreeable" matters, say, collectivization or the Gulag, made these intellectuals more effective politically.

Mistaken ideas about communist systems included the belief that they brought about spectacular material progress without the pain, deprivation, and alienation associated with modernization under capitalism. Peter Worsley, an English social scientist, was impressed by "the Chinese attempt to transform human values and personal relationships at the level of everyday life and to challenge assumptions that certain modes

87. E. J. Hobsbawm, "Intellectuals and Communism," in Mount, *Communism*, pp. 116–17.

of behavior are naturally 'entailed' under conditions of industrial life . . . that some form of class systems is inevitable . . .
[and] that the attractiveness of material gratifications must, in
the end, reassert itself."[88] It was one of the cardinal misconceptions—not limited to Mao's China—that social equality was
energetically and successfully pursued by communist regimes
and that if there was any inequality left, it was based on true
merit. The privileges of the *nomenklatura* were unknown.

It was also widely believed that the standard of living of
the masses hugely improved in each of these countries, resulting from the farsighted policies of their governments. Paul
Samuelson, the distinguished American economist, reportedly
believed, as of 1976, that "it was a vulgar mistake to think that
most people in Eastern Europe are miserable." Galbraith wrote
in 1984 that the Soviet economy made "great material progress in recent years . . . one sees it in the appearance of solid
well-being of the people on the streets."[89]

A particular source of admiration was the belief that social
problems plaguing Western, capitalist countries such as crime,
alcoholism, drug addiction, poverty, family disintegration, ra-
cial or sexual discrimination, and ethnic strife were being sub-
stantially reduced or completely eliminated in these societies.

The one-party system, far from suggesting lack of choice
and alternatives, was proof of the legitimacy of these governments; few wondered about the plausiblity of 99 percent plu-
ralities the uncontested official candidates garnered.

Those who found virtue in the domestic political-social
arrangements of communist systems also believed that their
foreign policies were benign and peaceful, that aggression was

---

88. *Inside China* (London: A. Lane, 1975), p. 20.
89. Both of these observations were quoted in *Freedom Review*, July–
August 1992, p. 6.

alien to them, and that they became defensive or bellicose only when threatened by Western hostility. George Kennan, who otherwise had no illusions about the nature of the Soviet system, believed that its leaders were "to some extent victims . . . of the idelogy on which they have been reared, but shaped far more importantly by the discipline of the responsibility they . . . have borne as rulers of a great country . . . men more seriously concerned to preserve the present limits of their political power . . . than to expand those limits . . . whose motivation is essentially defensive."[90]

Only a handful of those who harbored the misconceptions sampled above subsequently admitted their errors publicly.

GRASPING REALITY

Not all Western views of communist systems were permeated and shaped by ignorance, illusion, wishful thinking, or misplaced sympathy. There were numerous well-informed Western intellectuals, among them academic specialists, writers, and journalists who suceeded in identifying the key characteristics of communist systems, had few illusions about their superiority over Western societies, and were willing to make moral judgments of their defects without compromising their analytic faculties. It is hard to say what they had in common, what saved them from illusions, and why they were (or became) immune to identifying communist systems and movements with progress, humane modernization, the triumph of social justice, and a new sense of community. Some were former supporters or sympathizers who benefited from an inside view of the phenomenon they described and were

90. Quoted in Paul Hollander, *The Survival of the Adversary Culture* (New Brunswick, N.J.: Transaction Publishers, 1988), pp. 34–35.

transformed from admirers into critics. As far as the Soviet Union is concerned they include Rosa Luxemburg, Emma Goldman, Victor Serge, the contributors to the volume *The God That Failed* (Louis Fisher, André Gide, Arthur Koestler, Ignazio Silone, Stephen Spender, and Richard Wright), Albert Camus, Milovan Djilas, Howard Fast, Eugene Genovese, Doris Lessing, Wolfgang Leonhard, André Malraux, and Bertram Wolfe.

Among academic specialists who made lasting contributions to the understanding of communist systems and especially the Soviet Union, many were of East-Central European origin. They, or their families, had personal experience of the systems they left behind. Among them are Thomas Aczel, Zbigniew Brzezinski, Alexander Dallin, Alexander Gerschenkron, Jerzy Gliksman,[91] Peter Kenez, Leszek Kolakowski, Leo Labedz, Walter Laqueur, Tibor Meray, Czeslaw Milosz, Richard Pipes, Leonard Schapiro, Adam Ulam, and Ferenc Vali.

Equally illustrious contributions have been made by other scholars who did not have an East-Central European background, such as Raymond Aron (the first to address systematically the illusions of Western intellectuals about both the Soviet systems and Marxism),[92] Frederick Barghoorn, Raymond Bauer, Cyril Black, Abram Bergson, Walter Connor, Robert Conquest, Robert Daniels, Merle Fainsod, Lewis Feuer, Alex Inkeles, Nathan Leites,[93] Barrington Moore, David Powell and Peter Reddeway.

---

91. *Tell the West* (New York: Gresham Press, 1948). A particularly informative volume, as it combines the sympathizer's perspective (including political tourism) with experience of his subsequent incarnation as an inmate of the Gulag.

92. *The Opium of Intellectuals* (London, 1957).

93. In this section I am citing works that have either been forgotten or

Various aspects of Mao's China were revealed in the studies of Maria Chang, Michael Frolic, Merle Goldman, A. James Gregor, Chalmers Johnson, Simon Leys, Lucian Pye, Robert Scalapino, Ezra Vogel, and Martin Whyte. Steven Mosher provided a revealing study of Western misconceptions of China.[94]

The understanding of communist Cuba was greatly advanced by Alfred Cuzan, Jorge Dominguez, Rene Dumont, Jorge Edwards,[95] Mark Falcoff, Hugh Thomas, Irving Louis Horowitz,[96] William Ratliff, and Jacobo Timmerman.[97] Shirley Christian, Robert Leiken, and William Ratliff were among the few who dispelled many illusions about Sandinista Nicaragua. Per Ahlmark of Sweden has been engaged for decades in fighting the widespread and deeply rooted misconceptions about contemporary communist systems that prevailed among his fellow intellectuals in Scandinavia (his books have yet to appear in English). Anthony Daniels, insufficiently known in this country, has brilliantly captured the quality of life in the smaller communist states that survived after 1989.[98]

There has been far less public reassessment among the supporters of the second-generation communist systems than among former devotees of the Soviet Union at earlier times; those more recently disillusioned kept their revised judgments to themselves for the most part. The important exceptions in-

---

never received the amount of attention they deserve. They include Nathan Leites, *A Study of Bolshevism* (Glencoe, Ill.: Free Press, 1953).

94. Steven Mosher, *China Misperceived* (New York: Basic Books, 1990). See also his *Broken Earth: The Rural Chinese* (New York: Free Press, 1983) and *Journey to the Forbidden China* (New York: Free Press, 1985).

95. *Persona Non Grata* (New York: Paragon House, 1977).

96. I. L. Horowitz edited the volume *Cuban Communism* (New Brunswick, N.J.: Transaction Publishers), a major collection of scholarly studies of Castro's Cuba that had nine editions between 1970 and 1998.

97. *Cuba: A Journey* (New York: Knopf, 1990).

98. *Utopias Elsewhere* (New York: Crown, 1991).

clude Paul Berman, Eldridge Cleaver, Maurice Halperin,[99] David Horowitz, Julius Lester, Ronald Radosh, Orville Schell, and Susan Sontag.

Numerous other distinguished Western intellectuals also understood communist systems without the benefit of either prior sympathy for them or being born in one of the countries concerned. They include Malcolm Muggeridge, George Orwell, Jean Francois Revel, and Bertrand Russell, who early on took a good measure of Lenin and the system he was creating.[100]

At last are the large number of former citizens of communist systems who left these countries—refugees, defectors, and expellees—whose accounts greatly enriched our knowledge of these countries but whose work would require separate and extensive treatment not possible here.

The findings of those who understood communist systems converged in several respects. They all discerned and described the vast, delegitimizing discrepancy between the official ideals and promises and the actual character of the social-political institutions and systems that were created. It is important to note that, despite the huge gap between theory and practice, ideals and realities, the ideas of Marxism and Leninism were not without responsibility for the political-institutional realities these systems created, having provided initial inspiration and theoretical assurances for those who came to rule.

Communist systems, no matter how different in their historical background, economic development, and geographic

99. See his *The Rise and Decline of Fidel Castro* (Berkeley: University of California Press, 1972); *The Taming of Fidel Castro* (Berkeley: University of California Press, 1981); and *Return to Havana* (Nashville, Tenn.: Vanderbilt University Press, 1994).

100. Bertrand Russell, *Bolshevism: Practice and Theory* (New York: Harcourt, Brace and Howe, 1920).

location, shared several defining attributes and flaws. They were all repressive, often totalitarian, because they attempted to radically restructure social institutions and reshape human nature and by doing so force people into patterns of behavior that were profoundly uncongenial to them. The repression was also a consequence of an intolerance inspired by the lofty goals and a determined attachment to power they justified.

Most of these societies remained largely backward economically apart from the military realm:[101] they were capable of producing long-range missiles and tanks but not enough food and consumer goods. They inflicted a vast amount of propaganda on their people that was designed to redefine the social realities their citizens experienced; these regimes tried (in vain) to "to defeat experience with words."[102] Most of these systems for most of their existence were dominated by the unchecked power of leaders surrounded by grotesque and obligatory cults.

These systems also failed to eradicate the problems and defects whose existence they deplored in capitalist societies: crime, alcoholism, prostitution, bureaucracy, environmental destruction, as well as the kind of alienation associated with life in modern, urban, secular societies. As John Clark and Aaron Wildavski pointed out, "every evil attributed to capitalism turn[ed] up under socialism"; these systems, which were "to alter human relations from selfish isolation to altruistic

101. Czechoslovakia, Hungary, and East Germany were more consumer oriented and developed economically; Hungary and Poland during the 1970s and 1980s were also less repressive.
102. Dariusz Tolczyk, *See No Evil: Literary Cover-Ups and Discoveries of the Soviet Camp Experience* (New Haven, Conn.: Yale University Press, 1999), p. 3, xxi.

communitarianism . . . created a caricature of capitalism in which everyone was forced to fend for themselves."[103]

As was also shown by various authors, the abolition of the market and private ownership of the means of production led to the loss of productivity, the decline of the work ethic, and the chronic inability to meet consumer needs; central planning proved incapable of anticipating the needs of the economy and contributed to inefficiency, bureaucracy, and corruption.[104]

Those who understood, through careful study or personal experience, life under these systems also learned that they were overwhelmed by the unintended consequences of their policies. The centralized economy did not lead to efficiency except in meeting the needs of the military; indoctrination did not produce loyalty in the long run; repression stifled initiative; demands of conformity interfered with learning about and rectifying the varieties of institutional malfunctioning; "public property" did not inspire respect; low wages and salaries undermined incentives for work; ethnic tensions were not eliminated, only suppressed. Last but not least every communist system failed to achieve its proudest claim: the creation of a new, more ethical human being.

A major lesson, as Arthur Koestler formulated it a long time ago, has been that "man is a reality, mankind an abstraction; that men cannot be treated as units in operations of polit-

103. *The Moral Collapse of Communism* (San Francisco: Institute of Contemporary Studies, 1990), pp. 16–17, 311, 336.

104. A useful and not widely known contribution to understanding the failure of planning and its political consequences is Ferenc Feher, Agnes Heller, and Gyorgy Markus, *Dictatorship over Needs* (New York, 1983).

ical arithmetic . . . that the end justifies the means only within very narrow limits."[105]

Two major conclusions may be drawn from the Western misjudgments sketched above. The first is that disaffection from one's own society may seriously endanger understanding other social-political systems and can lead to their profound misapprehension. The second is that the attempt to judge the virtues and vices of any society must take into account the extent to which it accommodates or frustrates what seem to be basic human needs and dispositions. Much remains to be learned about the precise nature of these needs, but the collapse of communism should stimulate their better understanding since arguably it occurred because of the determination to ignore them.

105. Koestler in Richard Crossman, ed., *The God That Failed* (New York: Bantam, 1950), p. 60.

INDEX